HOW DOES IT GET THERE?

WESTMINSTER PRESS BOOKS

BY

GEORGE SULLIVAN

How Does It Get There?
How Do They Build It?
How Do They Run It?
More How Do They Make It?
How Do They Grow It?
How Do They Make It?

HOW
DOES IT GET THERE?

by
GEORGE SULLIVAN

THE WESTMINSTER PRESS

Philadelphia

BOOK DESIGN BY
DOROTHY ALDEN SMITH

PUBLISHED BY THE WESTMINSTER PRESS®
PHILADELPHIA, PENNSYLVANIA

PRINTED IN THE UNITED STATES OF AMERICA

Library of Congress Cataloging in Publication Data

Sullivan, George, 1927–
　　How does it get there?

　　SUMMARY: Describes the methods and equipment used to solve some modern and unusual cargo problems, such as shipping zoo animals or delivering mail to the bottom of the Grand Canyon.
　　Bibliography: p.
　　1. Transportation—Juvenile literature.
　　2. Freight and freightage—Juvenile literature.
　　[1. Freight and freightage.　2. Transportation]
　　I. Title.
TA1149.S94　　　　　　　380.5′2　　　　　　73–10345
ISBN 0–664–32535–1

CONTENTS

1

THE BIG STEEL BOX

A MANUFACTURER of television sets had a problem. The company's wood cabinets were handcrafted by skilled artisans in West Germany, while the electronic components were assembled in Decatur, Illinois. The problem: how to get them together quickly, safely, and on time.

Or take the case of the vanishing timepieces. An American wristwatch manufacturer found a booming market for his product in Western Europe, but every time he sent a shipment overseas large quantities of his product were stolen.

Finally, consider the plight of a Florida orange juice processor who wanted to get bottled juice from Bradenton, Florida, to London, England, fast and without breakage. In his first attempt the cases stayed so long on the New York docks that the juice went bad. The second time he tried, the juice got to England quickly enough but about one bottle out of every four was broken during unloading.

The solution in each case was the same: a container, a big steel box about the size of a railroad freight car. Shipments are loaded into the container, locked and sealed for protection, and not unsealed or unlocked until they reach their destination.

The manufacturer of television sets loaded the West German-made cabinets into containers and shipped them to Decatur. There the electronic components were installed, and the containers were reloaded with the finished television sets and shipped to distribution centers throughout the United States.

Factory-locked containers thwarted the pilferers who were helping themselves to the wristwatches. As for the orange juice processor, he simply loaded crated gallons of his product into specially insulated containers, saw them trucked a few miles north to Tampa, where they were loaded aboard a waiting container ship and then were sped to Europe.

Nowadays, when you ask the question, "How does it get there?" the answer almost always is, "By container." These sturdy corrugated metal

A "big steel box" is hoisted aboard a container ship

boxes have triggered a revolution in transportation, completely revising methods of moving and handling cargo that had gone unchanged for over a century. Giant gantry cranes, odd-looking straddle trucks, computerized traffic controls, container ships that cross oceans at record speeds—all of these are parts of the revolution, but at the heart of it is the big steel box.

One end of the container is a double-door opening. Swing the doors open and walk in. It is like entering a long, narrow room. The "ceiling" is 8 feet high. The "walls" are 8 feet apart. The largest containers are 40 feet in length. A container of this size—8′ × 8′ × 40′—weighs 6,300 pounds. It can hold a cargo load of more than 50,000 pounds.

In the early years of container use, the boxes came in many sizes and shapes. This led to chaos at some terminals, because it was difficult for shippers to interchange containers with

any degree of efficiency. The logjam was broken in 1965 when the International Organization of Standards said that containers had to be of specific sizes—8 feet wide, 8 feet high, and 20, 30, or 40 feet in length. Later the IOS agreed to a fourth length of 10 feet.

Actually, there are several different types of containers. The "workhorse" container is the steel box. Shippers refer to it as a dry-cargo container. It is used for machinery and manufactured goods of every type.

Bulk containers are similar to dry-cargo containers in outward appearance, but inside they're different, for they contain a second container that

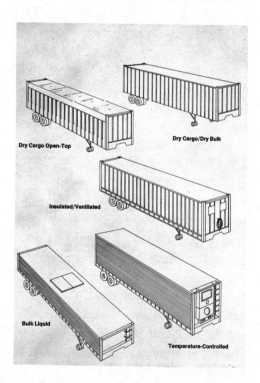

Principal types of containers

fits snugly inside the outer one. Dry-bulk commodities—dry chemicals, cement, flour, and plastic resins—are piped under pneumatic pressure into the inner container. There they are kept free of moisture and contamination.

Ice cream, frozen foods, and many perishable foods travel in "reefers," which are containers with built-in refrigeration units. Temperatures inside such containers can be regulated from a low of $-150°$ F., a necessity for frozen meat, to a high of $60°$ F., which is required on some winter days to protect strawberries and citrus fruits from the freezing cold.

With transporting most fruits and vegetables, it is usually only necessary to insulate or ventilate them. With an insulated container the temperature of the cargo at loading is maintained throughout the trip, despite extremes of heat or cold that might be encountered en route. Ventilated containers permit fresh air to circulate around the cargo. This helps to keep the shipment fresh.

There are containers for liquids too. Spirits and liquid chemicals ride in such "tanks." About half the height of a dry-cargo container, containers of this type carry as much as 5,000 gallons of liquid. Thanks to special tank-cleaning facilities at major terminals, a container that carried molasses one day can be used for grapefruit juice the next, with no fear of contamination.

What's so important about con-tainers is that they can be moved by sea, rail, highway, or air, or by any combination of these, on a single trip. Overseas shipments used to be made from port to port. If you happened to be a manufacturer of electronic equipment in Chicago and you wanted to send your product to England, you first had to arrange to get the shipment to New York or some other East Coast port. You then had to make arrangements with the steamship line to get the shipment across the Atlantic.

Container shipping has changed all of this. Now shipments go from door to door. From your headquarters in Chicago you simply call a local representative of the steamship company and ask him to deliver an empty container to your warehouse. You pack it, lock it, and seal it. The steamship company arranges to have it picked up, transported to the port city, loaded aboard the ship, and delivered to the destination you have specified. This means that it is now possible to ship directly from anywhere in mid-America to Europe, even to cities in *mid*-Europe.

"Look upon the container as a portable part of a ship," says an executive of one steamship line. "It can be moved about, loaded and unloaded, away from the ship, and then placed back aboard at the appropriate time."

Containers have made for a whole new generation of merchant ships—container ships. They are fast, safe, and efficient. They treat cargo better than some lines used to treat passengers.

A modern container ship

The *American Lancer,* one of a fleet of container ships operated by United States Lines, is typical. It is just over 700 feet in length. It travels at a speed of 22 knots, which puts most European ports only six days away from East Coast cities of the United States.

Ships like the *American Lancer* take containers of every type—dry-cargo containers, ventilated containers, and those with open tops. There are "plug-in" facilities for refrigerator containers. When locked into a cargo hold, the containers cannot shift, slide, or tilt. The system works in much the same way that a molded egg carton holds eggs. In addition, the ship is equipped with a special antiroll stabilizer that helps to prevent rocking and pitching in storms and heavy seas.

Containers that are stored on the open deck are just as secure as hold-loaded cargo. Ingenious linkages and fasteners prevent shifting.

During the early 1970's, the trend was toward bigger, faster container ships. The *Sea-Land Galloway,* which began operation between New York and Europe in 1972, ranks as the fastest cargo ship in the world. If it leaves New York on a Friday morning, it

10

arrives in Rotterdam on the evening of the following Tuesday.

The *Sea-Land Galloway* is more than one sixth of a mile in length. It carries over a thousand containers. Two such vessels are now in transatlantic service, and six are in service between Pacific ports and the Far East.

For every container berth on a ship, at least three containers are required. One is aboard the ship while it is at sea, a second (for use on the next voyage)

The Sea-Land Galloway, *fastest cargo ship in the world*

is at the customer's warehouse being loaded, while the third (from the previous voyage) is being unloaded.

This means that for a ship with a 1,000-container capacity, 3,000 containers must be purchased. That's only the start of it, however. The average life of a container is estimated to be about one third the life of the ship that carries it, which means that a total of 9,000 containers are needed over the lifetime of a ship with a 1,000-container capacity. The steamship line can end up paying more for a ship's containers than the original cost of the vessel itself.

It was estimated that in December, 1972, some 450,000 containers were in use, and the number was expected to double before the end of the decade. To keep track of their containers, steamship lines rely on computers.

The computers operate 24 hours a day, 7 days a week, accepting, storing, and transmitting data on each box. "Where is my container now? When can I expect it to arrive at its destination?" These are the questions that shippers are constantly asking. Computers provide the answers instantly.

Computers also perform much of the paper work necessary in shipping goods across oceans. They print out bills of lading, the documents that acknowledge the receipt of goods for shipment. These and other documents are transmitted to the port city well before the ship carrying the related cargo arrives.

Modern container ports no more look like port facilities of the past than a sleek new automobile resembles Henry Ford's Model T. Gone are the wooden shed-covered piers. No longer do crews of longshoremen wrestle with cargo, loading it into nets piece by piece for hoisting aboard ships. Waterfront traffic jams caused by trucks lined up for unloading are becoming a thing of the past.

At a modern port, containers by the thousands are stacked neatly in 2- or 3-high tiers within a vast staging area. When a container is needed for loading aboard ship, it is picked up by a monster straddle truck or powerful forklift and delivered to a gantry crane. Big container ports have several gantrys.

Each crane travels up and down the dock on steel rails. It doesn't matter whether the container being loaded is 20 feet or 40 feet in length, or some size in between. The crane has spreaders that telescope in and out electrically, adapting to the size of the load in the same way that a pair of hands adjusts to a carton of a particular size. It takes only a minute for a crane to put a container on board or remove it. An entire ship can be loaded or unloaded in less than a day. It used to take three days.

Automation characterizes every phase of the operation. When a truck pulls up with a container for one of the ships, the driver doesn't even have to leave his cab in order to find out where to deliver it. He hands over the documents through the cab window to an official at the entry gate. The documents are sped by pneumatic tube to a traffic control center. Within a minute, the driver's orders come back through the tube.

At some terminals, an electronic scanner at the entrance gate "reads" small colored strips that have been affixed to the container's front and sides. These strips are a coded version of the container's identification number. The scanner transmits the signal it receives to a computer, which then adds the container to the terminal records. When a container leaves the terminal, the computer is instructed to subtract it from the inventory.

One company double-checks its records by the use of a portable scanner that is mounted atop a small truck. Every two hours, the truck is driven up and down the long rows of parked containers, its scanner focused on the coded labels. This provides an up-to-the-minute container inventory.

An aerial view of the ship facilities and container-staging areas at Port Elizabeth

The port of New York is America's container capital. It embraces a great pie-shaped area of water about 50 miles across, with the Statue of Liberty at its center. Known officially as the New York–New Jersey Port District, it offers more than 200 piers with space enough for almost 400 ships. Container terminals have been constructed in Brooklyn, Staten Island, Port Newark, and Port Elizabeth. They handle 96.8 percent of all shipping entering New York harbor.

Manhattan Island used to be the focal point of harbor traffic. It was ringed with piers and dock facilities. But cramped Manhattan doesn't have the enormous amount of space required to store containers. There are still many piers standing in Manhattan, but only a handful of them are used for ocean cargo.

The same is true of the Delaware River in Philadelphia and of Boston harbor. Terminal facilities for these ports have been shifted in recent years to outlying areas, where there is plenty of room for container storage and easy access to express highways. In these cities as well as in Manhattan, ancient and decaying areas are being used for parks, office buildings, and apartment projects.

No one knows for sure exactly how or when the concept of containerization began. It is known that the nation's railroads played an important role in the development of containers and their widespread use.

It all started sometime in the 1800's.

Somebody, a person whose name has been lost to history, decided it was too much work to unload a wagon and reload its contents into a railroad car. So he drove the loaded wagon up onto a railroad flatcar, made it secure, and then had it transported to its destination. The horses were left behind, of course, and other horses obtained later.

So the farm wagon was the first container, and farmers were the first container users. Traveling circuses also

Straddle trucks and powerful forklifts are used to deliver containers from staging areas to loading cranes

UNION PACIFIC RAILROAD

13

utilized the container. It was too much of a hazard to unload and reload lions, tigers, and such at every stop, so their cages were fitted with wheels and simply rolled onto flatcars for shipment from one city to another.

Late in the 1920's the railroads began hauling truck trailers on flatcars. No one paid much attention to the idea at the time because the number hauled was small.

The service didn't begin to achieve real importance until the 1950's, when it came to be known as "piggybacking." A significant development in the growth of piggybacking came in 1954, when the Interstate Commerce Commission ruled that railroads could haul trailers on flatcars without holding a motor carrier certificate. In other rulings handed down later, the railroads

A gantry crane lifts a container into place
UNITED STATES LINES

14

were given permission to handle trailers owned by themselves, by trucklines, or by shippers. Piggybacking mushroomed in growth during the years that followed.

Before the idea of piggybacking was very old, railroads took it a step farther. As the concept had originated, the highway trailer complete with its wheels was carried on a flatcar. The next stage was to develop a highway trailer with removable wheels.

A trailer of this type was backed up to a special flatcar with a turntable. After the trailer's road wheels were unhooked, the trailer was rotated on the turntable and locked into position. The wheels were left behind and provisions were made to secure another set at the destination.

The jump from a highway trailer with removable wheels to a metal container designed for shipboard stowage was a very short one. The chief difference between the two is in weight, containers being considerably lighter. Containers also have a lower center of gravity, permitting them to be loaded and unloaded with greater speed.

Container ships are not a new development either. They date from 1957. In October that year, the first fully containerized vessel, *The Gateway City,* after being loaded at Port Newark, headed south to Miami and then on to Tampa and Houston. Throngs of official well-wishers greeted the ship everywhere. Congressman Herbert C. Bonner of North Carolina, then chairman of the House Merchant Marine Committee, called the vessel "the greatest advance for the merchant marine of our time."

During the 1960's the use of containers was largely experimental. Ships that were originally built for other purposes—tankers or cargo vessels—were converted or enlarged to haul containers. But such vessels were not used in transoceanic service. They transported goods from one port in the United States to another—from Port Newark to Houston, for example, or from New York to coastal Florida ports.

But with the advent of the container ship, shipping firms began to extend their horizons. During the early 1960's, container vessels began regularly scheduled service between New York and San Juan and between Seattle and Anchorage. By the middle of the decade, container ships were making frequent North Atlantic crossings from New York to Rotterdam and Bremen, Germany's chief port city. Container ship service to the Far East came next: the Seattle to Yokohama route was opened in 1968, and soon after, Hong Kong, Taiwan, and the Philippines were added to the list. During the Vietnam war, container ships in service from Pacific Coast ports to Camranh Bay and Saigon carried supplies and equipment to United States military forces.

Container ship service between East Coast ports (Port Elizabeth, Boston, Baltimore, and other ports) and the Far East (ports in Japan, Korea, Hong Kong, and the Philippines) began in mid-1971.

Containerization has produced many changes in the way goods are moved between continents. Because containers can be hauled by ship, train, or truck with equal facility, European goods bound for the West Coast of the United States are now moving through East Coast ports and across the country by rail. They used to go through the Panama Canal. What's happening is that the United States is being used as a "land bridge."

The "land bridge" idea is also being utilized in the movement of goods between Japan and Europe. Japanese electronic parts, film, and other products of high value are packed into containers, shipped to Seattle, hauled by train to New York, and then transferred aboard ship again for transport to European ports. Goods from Japan to Europe used to be shipped west through the Suez Canal, a 44-day voyage. The door-to-door "land bridge" across the United States requires about 28 days.

Many foreign shippers used to use the St. Lawrence Seaway, the canal and river route along the St. Lawrence River between Montreal and Lake Ontario, when sending goods from East Coast ports to the Midwest. But many have found that it is more efficient to load their containers on flatcars and ship by rail. "The St. Lawrence Seaway is becoming just a lake again as far as general cargo is concerned," says one shipper. (The Seaway will continue to

A containerized freight crosses the "land bridge"

play an important role in the shipment of bulk cargo, such as grain and petroleum.)

Constant change and innovation have marked container shipping since its earliest days. One of the most significant recent developments is the LASH ship, LASH being an acronym for *L*ighter (a lighter is another name for a barge) *A*board *Sh*ip. LASH vessels are capable of handling not merely individual containers but barges full of them. Each LASH ship is equipped with a 500-ton gantry crane mounted on rails that run the full length of the ship. The crane picks up a barge, hoists it over the stern, and stows it in a hold or on the deck. Each LASH vessel can transport 63 barges.

Each barge holds several containers, the number depending upon their size. So each barge is actually a supersize container.

There is a gain in efficiency for the shipper because of the increased size of the basic transport unit. But that's not the only advantage. Since each LASH ship is equipped with its own crane, vessels of this type don't have to tie up at a dock for loading or unloading. They can stay offshore, outside the port. Tugs deliver barges to the ship or pick up barges from it.

This can result in an important saving for the shipowner. The average cargo ship on a transatlantic run spends about one half of its time in port, and much of this time is spent waiting for dock space. On a recent voyage to the Mediterranean, the LASH *Italia* stopped at Barcelona for 8 hours instead of the usual 24; it spent 9 hours off Genoa, usually a 2-day stop.

A LASH ship from the United States can cover the entire Mediterranean

16

Lighters (foreground) *cluster about the LASH* Espana

trade route and return in 33 days. A conventional ship covering the same route and faced with the problem of clogged ports takes 54 days. Thus, LASH ships offer shippers considerable saving.

The first LASH vessel was developed by a New Orleans naval architectural firm, built in Japan, and put into operation in 1969. Named the *Acadia Forest* and operated by the International Paper Company, it picked up barges loaded with paper products from the company's mills at Vicksburg and Natchez, Mississippi, sailed down the Mississippi River to New Orleans, and then on to Europe. The ship is still in operation.

Port Newark, Norfolk, Providence, Boston, and Philadelphia are among the ports from which LASH ships now operate. They carry American-made agricultural equipment, automobile parts, machine tools, computers, and food products to Europe. On the return voyage, they transport from Italy such products as canned tomatoes, shoes, and marble slabs, and from other Mediterranean countries nuts, raisins, dates, and figs.

Bigger and bigger LASH ships have already begun to make their appearance on the nation's waterways. The *Doctor Lykes,* the biggest general cargo ship to fly the American flag, went into operation in 1972, steaming between New Orleans and Europe. With a single hoist, the mighty elevator system of this LASH ship can lift barges containing loads weighing as much as 1700 tons.

The United States is presently involved in a major maritime construction effort, in which approximately $3 billion is to be spent. LASH ships are one important aspect of the program.

17

The Doctor Lykes, *biggest general cargo ship under the American flag*

"They've ushered in a new era in shipping," says one expert in the field. "They could be as important to the industry today as the Yankee clipper was to shippers in the nineteenth century."

LASH ships aren't the only significant development. Trailer ships are another. A trailer ship is capable of taking aboard and unloading vehicles hauling containerized freight in, a simple, speedy roll-on, roll-off operation. The need for a crane is eliminated.

Three land-based steel ramps connect to ramp openings on the starboard side of the trailer ship. Once they're in place, the parade begins. Trucks rumble aboard pulling dry-cargo containers, bulk containers, and reefers. Red and green traffic lights regulate the traffic flow. Each vehicle is directed to one of the vessel's five decks, where it is secured into tie-down slots. The chassis portion is then detached and driven ashore to get another load.

When the trailer ship reaches its destination, the caravan reverses direction. As many as a thousand containers can be driven on and off in a single turnaround. The entire operation takes only twelve hours.

Besides transporting containers of conventional size and weight, trailer ships can also handle all types of outsize cargo. Shipments of 95-foot lengths of steel pipe, huge cranes, a 60-foot-long cooling tower, and giant earthmovers are driven on and off with

A trailer rolls off the trailer ship Ponce de Leon *in San Juan, Puerto Rico*

ease. "We carry anything on wheels" is the slogan of the leading trailer ship firm.

Another unique feature of the trailer ship is the speed—26 knots. Trailer ships on the run between New York and San Juan, Puerto Rico, make the trip in 60 hours, almost 50 percent faster than conventional ships.

Trailer ship service dates to 1968, the year that the *Ponce de Leon* began a weekly run between New York and Puerto Rico. By mid-1973, three trailer ships were in operation between East Coast ports and Puerto Rico. As for the future, on the drawing board are plans calling for trailer ships that are 50 percent larger than those in use today. These will be used in transoceanic service.

The most significant development in the construction of container ships may be taking place overseas. West German shipbuilders are turning out container vessels that utilize gas turbine engines instead of conventional steam or diesel propulsion units. It is claimed that gas turbines are more reliable over an extended period of time. But the big advantage with gas turbines is the saving in space; the engine room can be reduced by as much as 60 percent. The saved space is given over to container storage.

Some people say that the container revolution has only just begun. Many more changes are forecast. One study foresees the day when there will be only two or three major container ports

The future may see container delivery by helicopter

SIKORSKY AIRCRAFT

serving the East Coast of the United States. Other ports will be mere feeder ports, with barges and ships from these cities funneling cargo to the larger ones.

The automated container warehouse is another possible future development. Containers would be stacked in tall vertical tiers, and each summoned for loading by the press of a button. The idea, now in the first stages of development, would save as much as 80 percent of the space now given over to container marshaling yards. Research is being conducted on the ship-to-shore delivery of containers by helicopter and on huge container barges that would cross oceans underwater, unaffected by the wind and waves.

But even if none of these changes takes place, the container revolution has been profound and the industry has been transformed.

2

FIRST STEPS TOWARD SPACE

THE 252,950-MILE FLIGHT of an Apollo spacecraft to the moon at speeds of up to 25,000 miles an hour begins with a crawl, with a 3-mile, 3-hour trip from the assembly building to the launching pad. This brief and plodding journey requires the services of one of the world's most unusual vehicles.

Known as a crawler-transporter, it consists of a raised steel platform that is almost big enough to hold two bas-

ketball courts side by side. Once the towering Saturn V rocket and the Apollo spacecraft are aboard, the platform lumbers along on four double-track treads. These resemble tractor or bulldozer treads in everything but size; each is as big as a city bus, 10 feet high and 40 feet long.

The most remarkable statistic concerning the crawler-transporter has to do with the weight it can carry—12 million pounds. It could haul a Navy

The crawler-transporter dwarfs attendants standing nearby

destroyer or 50 railroad boxcars. In terms of carrying capacity, no other land-going vehicle approaches it.

The crawler-transporter is of fairly recent vintage. In the early stages of rocket engineering and space exploration, space vehicles were assembled right on the pad from which they were to be launched. But this technique wasn't practical in building and testing the Saturn V series of rockets.

One problem was location. The Kennedy Space Center, built on an 88,000-acre tract of land on Merritt Island, a vast marshland and primitively wild area off the coast of central Florida, is exposed to the constant ravages of wind, rain, and corrosive salt air. That's not all. From June through November, it is hurricane season there, and violent storms are frequent.

Engineers realized that they could not assemble a sophisticated spacecraft under such conditions. The protected environment that they required led to the construction of the vehicle-assembly building, an enormous concrete cube. The doorway of the vehicle-assembly building is 456 feet in height, tall enough to admit a 40-story skyscraper.

Once the concept of the vehicle-assembly building was agreed upon, engineers had to figure out a way of getting newly built rockets and their service towers to the launching pads. Not only did the mobile system have to be capable of carrying the staggering weight involved, but it had to be able to move to and from the launching site with some degree of speed. Suppose a rocket was in position for a launch and word came that a hurricane was bearing down on the Cape. The transport system would have to be capable of picking up the rocket and spacecraft and getting them back to the safety of the vehicle-assembly building before the storm struck.

Many modes of transportation were evaluated. A rail system was one of the first. A dual-track railway had been used in the Saturn I program at Cape Kennedy. This involved the transportation of a service structure that weighed less than a million pounds. But in the case of the Saturn V and its service tower, the load was so much greater—11 million pounds greater—that it would have required a railway and railbed of completely different design. Studies showed the cost to be prohibitive.

A barge and canal system was investigated next. Engineers found that the barge would have to be of impractical size. Indeed, it would resemble a floating football field. Imagine the type of canal a barge of this size would require. One engineer estimated that it would have to be at least 150 feet wide. Digging and then maintaining such a waterway would be an expensive proposition, requiring scores of workers on a full-time basis. Before long, the barge concept was rejected too. Transport systems involving huge rubber rollers and giant pneumatic tires were also ruled impractical.

The crawler-transporter is a first cousin to power shovels like this one

Early in 1962, engineers at Cape Kennedy became aware of the huge power shovels that were being used in strip-mining operations. These great jawed scoops rumbled from one seam or outcropping of coal to the next on giant crawler treads. While these machines would never win any speed contests, they moved fast enough to be practical for the transport system being sought at Cape Kennedy.

One of these stripping shovels, manufactured by the Marion Power Shovel Co., Inc., of Marion, Ohio, known as the Marion 6360, was, at one time, the world's largest mobile land machine.

Its dipper was big enough (18′ × 24′ × 24′) to scoop up a dozen school buses in a single pass, and so powerful it could handle 270 tons of dirt and rock without straining. Yet even the Marion 6360 was only about one sixth the size of the proposed crawler-transporter.

Increasing the carrying capacity of the vehicle wasn't the only problem that the engineers faced. The machine had to be able to keep both the rocket and its service tower level as they were borne up the slope at the foot of the launching pad. Strip-mining shovels lacked this leveling capability.

One by one the problems were solved. The leveling system in the crawler-transporter is so efficient that when the vehicle begins climbing the 5 percent grade at the approach to the launching pad, the tip of the space vehicle, 363 feet above the crawler platform, drifts from the vertical by only a few inches.

Two crawler-transporters were ordered. They cost, according to officials of the National Aeronautics and Space Administration, "under 15 million." The first of the vehicles went into operation in 1965.

Two huge diesel engines power the transporters. Each one is capable of generating 2,750 horsepower, and each requires about 75 gallons of diesel fuel for every mile the transporter covers.

The number of men required to operate a crawler-transporter varies with the load. When it travels without any cargo, an eleven-man crew is needed. Once the rocket and the service structure are aboard and the transporter heads down the crawlerway, sixteen men are required. The number of crewmen needed rises to twenty-two when the rocket and launcher are being loaded or unloaded.

Loading takes place within the vehicle-assembly building. The crawler-transporter slips into place beneath the upright rocket and spacecraft. Then the vehicle's 16 hydraulic jacks —4 on each corner—raise the rocket from the pedestals on which it rests. Once the rocket has been secured to the platform, the doors of the building open to allow the transporter and its cargo to leave.

Moving at a snail's pace, the vehicle travels a specially built roadway, or, as it is called, a crawlerway. As wide

Leaving the vehicle-assembly building, the crawler-transporter begins the 3-mile trip to the launching pad

as an 8-lane highway with a 50-foot median strip, the crawlerway is capable of bearing a load in excess of 18¼ million pounds, which is the combined weight of the rocket, the spacecraft, and the crawler-transporter itself.

The roadbed for the crawlerway, composed of layers of fill and lime rock, is 8 feet thick. It has been capped with 8 inches of Alabama river rock and given an asphalt sealer topping.

When the crawler-transporter arrives at the launching pad it sets the rocket down on the pad. It then delivers a service tower. This tower has five circular work platforms that close around the rocket.

Working from these platforms, technicians load the first stage of the rocket with kerosene fuel and liquid oxygen. Into the second and third stages go liquid hydrogen and liquid oxygen. When the tanks of the spacecraft are filled to capacity, and engineers and technicians have begun the tense countdown, the crawler-transporter moves the service tower away from the pad, its final task before blast-off.

The two crawler-transporters at Cape Kennedy are going to be kept

The crawlerway to the launching pad resembles a superhighway

NASA

busy for many years to come. Both are to be used in hauling rockets and space vehicles in the Skylab and Space Shuttle programs, scheduled for the late 1970's.

3

THE SEA GIANTS

IMAGINE A TANKER so long that the Empire State Building could be laid on its deck and there would be only a few feet of overhang. Its storage tanks hold enough oil to keep Chicago running for four days.

Such a ship is no fantasy. It is the *Nisseki Maru,* and it travels the sea-lanes between Japan and the Persian Gulf. When the ship was delivered to its owners in September, 1971, following construction in Kure, Japan, the 372,698-ton vessel ranked as the biggest structure man had ever put together and expected to move.

While the *Nisseki Maru* has since lost that billing to an even bigger tanker, the ship is still recognized as a seagoing colossus. Everything about it suggests bigness. The vessel is almost a quarter of a mile in length; the bridge is 1,000 feet from the bow.

Fully loaded, the *Nisseki Maru* requires water 88 feet deep in order to navigate, more than twice the displacement of the world's biggest passenger liners. On each of its nine yearly trips from the Middle East to Japan, the *Nisseki Maru* carries 120 million gallons of crude oil, 18 times as much as the biggest tanker afloat twenty years ago.

The *Nisseki Maru* is one of a generation of supertankers, vessels of 250,000 tons or larger. The world's oil companies are ordering supertankers by the dozens.

The supertanker Universe Iran—*327,000 tons, 1,135 feet long, and with several acres of deck space, somewhat smaller than the* Nisseki Maru

GULF OIL COMPANY

25

The closing of the Suez Canal in 1967, a casualty of the bitter strife in the Middle East, helped to trigger the trend to transporting crude oil by supertanker. With the Canal shut down, oil from the Persian Gulf bound for Western Europe had to be hauled around the Cape of Good Hope at the southernmost tip of Africa, a trip of more than 11,000 miles. By way of the Suez Canal, the voyage was only one half that distance.

The petroleum industry realized that about twice as many tankers were going to be necessary to transport the same amount of oil. But rather than double the number of tankers, the in-

dustry chose to build dramatically bigger ones.

At the time of the closing of the Suez Canal, the term "supertanker" was used to describe vessels of 60,000 tons. They were the biggest in operation at the time because a 60,000-ton ship was the largest that could pass through the canal fully loaded. Since the new tankers weren't going to have to go through the canal, no limitation was placed on their size.

Actually, the word "supertanker" was first used in the early 1950's. It was applied at the time to vessels of about 25,000 tons. In 1958, the largest tanker afloat was 85,000 tons, while most new tankers were about 40,000 tons in size.

The closing of the Suez Canal was only part of the story. In May, 1970, Syrian forces punched a hole in the trans-Arabian pipeline, through which 470,000 barrels had been pumped daily to loading terminals in Lebanon.

A third reason that the demand for tankers has become acute has to do with the mushrooming demand for oil. In 1968, the world's total oil consumption stood at 39 million barrels a day. In 1970, it had risen to 42 milllion barrels daily, an 8 percent increase that no one had foreseen.

Japanese shipyards were the first to master the technique of building supertankers profitably and for years they held a virtual monopoly on their construction. Japan is still the world leader, but Sweden and France are building many of the new tankers on

The enormous carrying capacity of super-tankers is indicated by this view of the Esso Northumbria

Tankers take on crude oil at the port of Shuwaikh, Kuwait, on the Persian Gulf

order. Spanish shipyards became active in tanker construction in 1967, and Spain is where some of the biggest tankers are now being constructed.

The Japanese pioneered many of the construction techniques now used by other countries. For example, to lay out the shapes to be cut from each steel plate, workers with wooden patterns and measuring instruments used to laboriously chalk the outlines on each piece of steel. Other men with acetylene torches would then do the cutting. Now the job is done automatically. An electric eye follows a scaled-down drawing of the patterns, and a computer guides the cutting torches over the plates.

Another innovation involves prefabrication. Tankers used to be constructed from the keel up on an inclined slipway. When the vessel was completed, it would be allowed to slide down the slipway into the water. Not anymore. Supertankers are constructed in huge sections, called "blocks," which may weigh as much as 100 tons.

The blocks are assembled in sheds alongside a drydock, a huge empty basin that can be flooded with water. The bow is one section, the stern another, and parts of the hull and superstructure are others. As a block is completed, it is lifted into place by a powerful crane. This method enables workers to build and outfit several parts of a ship at one time.

Traditional methods of welding have gone the way of the clipper ship. Welding crews operate from mobile scaffolds that run on steel rails the length of the ship. The movement of the scaffolds is controlled by pushbuttons.

27

Japan leads all other nations in tanker construction. Here workers paint a tanker prior to launching at a Nagasaki shipyard

CONSULATE GENERAL OF JAPAN

When construction and assembly are completed, water is let in and the ship floats. The vessel is thus saved the strain of launching.

Japanese shipbuilders use their drydocks with the utmost efficiency. If a ship to be built is too long for the only available drydock, it is constructed in halves and the two pieces are joined later. Or suppose an 800-foot ship is under construction in a 1,200-foot drydock. Then the workers build a bow, a stern, or any other major section of a second ship in the leftover 400 feet.

During the early 1970's, Japan had approximately 30 major shipyards in operation. These offered five drydocks capable of building ships of over 200,-000 tons in size. Two new drydocks to handle the construction of tankers as large as 500,000 tons are expected to be ready by 1975.

One Japanese shipyard is capable of turning out tankers in the 350,000-ton class, from keel-laying to delivery, in ten months. With smaller tankers, only six months is required.

By 1973, Japan and some European nations had built about 200 supertankers. The United States had not built any. But American shipyards have awakened at last. Two supertankers are being built at what used to be the Brooklyn Navy Yard, where scores of warships were constructed during World War II.

The only other American facility capable of turning out supertankers is the Sparrows Point basin in the Baltimore harbor. This shipyard was opened in 1971. Three supertankers are being built there.

The enormous size of the supertankers makes for unusual navigational problems. Take the matter of starting and stopping. In the case of a ship such as the *Nisseki Maru,* it takes two hours for its 40,000-horsepower turbine to get the vessel up to its top speed of 15 knots.

A 70,000-ton tanker nears completion in the shipbuilding basin at Sparrows Point, Maryland. Ahead of it lies a section for a second 70,000-ton vessel

BETHLEHEM STEEL

Tanker and pier built on 1/25 scale give the navigator the "feel" of supertanker handling

Stopping can take as much as ten miles. To cut down the distance, the captain may "slalom," that is, steer alternately hard to the port side, then hard to the starboard. At the same time, he reverses the engines.

To compensate for their lack of maneuverability, supertankers have the most sophisticated navigational equipment available. Anticollision radar sounds a warning whenever another ship or obstacle is detected, and pinpoints its location electronically. If a collision should loom, the system charts a safe alternate course.

When a supertanker is attempting to maneuver in a narrow channel or near a pier, a sonar docking system reports the speed of the vessel's movement in any direction. The system is so sensi-

tive that it can detect a movement as slight as 1 foot per minute in a vessel 1,000 feet in length.

One oil company, as part of its collision prevention program, has established a navigational training school in the French Alps for its captains and officers. The school's purpose is to give the men the "feel" of the wind, waves, and currents that they will encounter at sea. Instead of a real ship and a real ocean, each trainee navigates a 40-foot fiberglass tanker model. It is powered by a one-half horsepower engine over a nine-acre man-made lake. There are model piers and navigation buoys, with everything scaled down on a one to twenty-five ratio.

When a prospective captain sits at the stern of his model vessel controlling the tiny engine, his eyes at pilot-house level, the effect is amazingly like the real thing. "My two weeks on the lake," said one trainee, "were worth twenty-five years at sea."

Despite such training methods and the many electronic safeguards, the operation of supertankers has not been trouble free. In 1970, the 207,000-ton *Marpessa,* sailing from England to pick up a load of crude oil from the Persian Gulf, blew up off the coast of West Africa. Only two weeks later, a similar blast ruptured the hull of the supertanker *Mactra* as the ship cruised the Mozambique Channel. The very next day an explosion blew apart the *Kong Maakon VII* off Liberia.

Were it not for the fact that these three ships were empty, the disasters could easily have been of much greater magnitude. When the *Torrey Canyon* ran aground off the southeast tip of England in 1967, the vessel was full of

Esso Nederland, *a 253,000-ton vessel, has a bow of distinctive design*

Persian crude oil that ended up on British beaches and raised havoc with marine life.

It was their very emptiness that caused these three ships to blow up, experts say. After a tanker unloads its crude oil, and the ship is far out at sea, its tanks are cleaned with jets of sea water. Vapors in the tanks combine with air to form an explosive mixture. Continued spraying generates static electricity. Under conditions such as these, the tiniest spark can trigger an explosion powerful enough to rip the ship apart.

Since the three disasters, cleaning procedures have been changed. Some tankers now carry inert gases, like nitrogen, in their empty tanks.

Environmentalists shudder at the thought of what would happen should a loaded tanker ever be involved in a collision or other accident at sea. But some experts claim that supertankers are *safer* than smaller ships. They argue that they are more seaworthy, less subject to stress and strain at sea. "A big tanker fully loaded is as sturdy as a brick church," says one spokesman for tanker interests.

Another argument is that because a few large tankers replace several small ones, fewer travel the seas and there is less chance of collision. And the fact that supertankers operate on other than conventional, crowded sea-lanes, and use terminal facilities not suited for other vessels, also reduces chances of collision.

It has been said that modern supertankers with all their sophisticated navigational equipment—their automatic radar, automatic piloting system, and automatic steering adjuster—run themselves. This is not completely true. From twenty-five to thirty-three men, the exact number depending on the size of the ship, are required.

Most crewmen belong to one of two categories: they are either responsible for the operation of the vessel or charged with maintaining it in running order. The operating personnel include the deckhands and seamen. The cooks and messmen, who handle the kitchen chores, and the radar and radio specialists are also operating personnel. Their work is supervised by the captain, or master.

The chief engineer is charged with the responsibility of keeping the vessel running, and his status is almost equal to that of the captain. The assistant engineers, firemen, oilers, and wipers report to the chief engineer.

Crew members experience a common problem in boredom. It takes less than 24 hours to load or unload the vessel. That means that a ship such as the *Nisseki Maru*, since it makes 9 trips a year, spends only 18 days out of every 365 in port. To help crewmen break the monotony of the days at sea, the ship has been fitted out with two recreation rooms and a nonskid, all-weather jogging track around the vessel's 4-acre deck. Crew members have cards, checkers and chess sets, and magazines, and there is a library of paperback books.

One petroleum company operates a fleet of supertankers each of which is equipped with a small swimming pool, a gymnasium, and a fully equipped darkroom for photography enthusiasts. The same company permits officers to take their wives along. Since tankers are not allowed to carry passengers, the wives sign on as "stewardesses."

Food is a very important matter, not only from a standpoint of nutrition and, consequently, crew performance but also as far as morale is concerned. A typical evening meal consists of a fish course, a meat course, vegetables, hot biscuits, dessert, and assorted beverages. Mealtime is a time of relaxation and socializing among the crewmen.

As one can imagine, a ship of 250,000 tons requires special port facilities. The 65 feet of water it needs in which to operate is twice the depth required by the average cargo ship. The supertanker needs a much wider area in which to turn and longer and stronger piers at which to tie up.

Ports in almost every part of the world are improving their facilities in order to be able to accommodate the supertankers. The port of Rotterdam, the world's busiest port, already able to handle ships of 250,000 tons, is engaged in a gigantic dredging and construction program to be ready for tankers of the 500,000-ton class and beyond. In Great Britain, the Welsh port of Milford Haven has dredged its main channel and now takes ships of up to 250,000 tons.

Supertankers are not noted for their ability to turn or maneuver. Here tugboats come to the aid of the Esso Malaysia

In Italy, Trieste has dug a waterway deep enough for ships of 200,000 tons. In Germany, Hamburg has constructed port facilities at the mouth of the Elbe River for tankers of up to 300,000 tons.

One oil company has built terminal facilities for its fleet of 326,000-ton tankers at Bantry Bay at Ireland's southern tip. Here the water is quiet and very deep—100 feet. Ships moor at a jetty that is fitted with pumping equipment, and the crude oil is quickly transferred to storage tanks onshore.

The Universe Ireland *unloads at Bantry Bay*

Later, smaller tankers haul the oil to refineries in Wales, Denmark, Holland, and Spain. A similar terminal in Okinawa serves Japan.

Late in 1972, there were approximately 50 superports in operation, including 14 in the Persian Gulf, many of them built by United States oil companies, and 19 in Japan. But the United States had none.

Three ports in the continental United States—Seattle, Los Angeles, and Long Beach—have water deep enough to handle supertankers. But no terminal facilities have been constructed.

The East and the Gulf Coasts, where the need is the greatest, have no deepwater ports, and it would be too costly to deepen existing channels. The alternative is to build offshore terminals in water that is deep enough to handle the big ships. These terminals would be connected by pipelines to the shore, and there would be loading facilities for smaller tankers and barges. Louisiana, Mississippi, and Texas are studying the idea of building offshore ports in the Gulf of Mexico.

Federal officials favor a site just outside Delaware Bay that leads to Philadelphia. But as efforts to build an offshore superport have been gathering momentum, so has the opposition. Environmentalists are concerned about oil spills and worry that the underwater pipeline might rupture. "During the late-summer hurricane season," says one spokesman for environmental interests, "an offshore terminal would be

like a time bomb. If it happened to 'explode,' the entire East Coast would be knee-deep in oil for months." Arguments of this type led the governor of Delaware to approve a law prohibiting the construction of a superport in Delaware Bay.

Public opposition stopped oil companies from building terminals for supertankers in the deepwater bays of Machiasport and Searsport, Maine. Proposals for mooring buoys off the East Coast, with floating connections to pipelines, have also been defeated.

Maybe the solution is a nearby foreign port. A terminal could be built in the Bahama Islands or in Canada. There the oil would be unloaded and transferred to smaller ships for delivery to the United States.

The Bahamian government favors such a terminal. So do some oil companies. They point out that the facility would be well located for transshipment of oil to both the East and the Gulf Coasts of the United States.

Canada has deepwater ports at five East Coast points. Two of them—St. John, New Brunswick, and Point Tupper, Nova Scotia—have harbors with depths that exceed 100 feet. Early in 1972, the *Universe Japan*, 326,000 tons, then the world's second largest ship, put into Point Tupper with 2.4 million barrels of crude oil from the Persian Gulf. There's a problem with Canadian ports, however, a financial one. The Canadian government has begun to levy surcharges on imported oil, which has cooled the enthusiasm of the oil companies for using and developing Canadian ports.

As of 1973, the United States was importing about 23 percent of its oil, with 3 percent of it coming from Middle East countries. But experts forecast that this figure is going to change drastically. By the early 1980's, the United States will be importing 40 to 60 percent of its oil, with the bulk of that coming from the Middle East. If, at that time, the United States still has no port to accommodate supertankers, it could be a superproblem.

Nothing has happened in recent years to halt the trend toward bigger and bigger supertankers. Early in 1973, when the 477,000-ton *Globtik Tokyo* began carrying crude oil from the Middle East to Japanese refineries, it ranked as the world's biggest ship.

But the title was one the ship didn't expect to have for very long.

French shipyards were already at work on two tankers, each 530,000 tons. These 1,370-foot vessels are scheduled for completion in 1976. Each is to cost approximately $80 million. They will haul crude oil between the Persian Gulf and two ports in France, Le Havre on the Atlantic Ocean and Fos on the Mediterranean Sea.

Supertankers as large as 1 million tons are planned. A vessel of this size would be 1,800 feet in length. Stand it on one end and it would be a full 250 feet taller than the Sears Tower, the world's tallest building. It would draw 100 feet of water. The supertankers of today may be the minitankers of tomorrow.

4

MAIL BY PAIL

CAPTAIN WILLIAM ADAMEK steered his doughty little boat directly toward the moving black steel hull of the Great Lakes steamer dead ahead and then veered to the right at the last split second. As the two vessels ran side by side, a crewman on the steamer lowered a white pail on which the words U.S. MAIL had been stenciled in black ink.

A deckhand on the small boat grabbed the bucket, placed a package of envelopes in it, signaled the crewman on the steamer, and watched as the bucket was hauled aboard. "O.K.," shouted the deckhand. At full throttle Captain Adamek pulled away, spinning the brass wheel.

The *J. W. Westcott II*, which represents the world's only mail service to moving ships, had just completed another one of its almost 14,000 annual deliveries. Operating up and down the Detroit River between Lake Erie and Lake St. Clair, one of the nation's busiest "thoroughfares," the *Westcott* serves the more than 10,000 crewmen of the lake steamers and freighters, which, unlike oceangoing vessels, don't have agents along the way to handle their mail.

The *Westcott*'s "pail mail" delivery service is one of the U.S. Postal Service's out-of-the-ordinary methods of reaching isolated addressees. There are countless others, each one as ingenious as the next. Indeed, when it comes to "getting it there," the U.S. Postal Service takes a back seat to no one.

The *Westcott*, however, is in a class by itself. It's the only boat in the world to have its own zip code—48222 (in case you care to write).

The *Westcott* also delivers newspapers, coffee, telegrams, and occasionally even a tardy seaman. But mail is the boat's most important cargo. In 1970 alone, the *Westcott* received and delivered nearly one million pieces of mail. During the eight months of the year that the Detroit River is navigable (not choked with ice), the boat works around the clock, seven days a week.

Television, radio, magazines, and newspapers have helped to spread the fame of the *Westcott*, and sailors have

Mail to be delivered in midriver goes aboard the Westcott

borne tales of the vessel around the world. The *Westcott* holds a special interest for stamp collectors. For the boat's first run of the season, which occurs right after the March thaw, philatelists prepare distinctively cacheted envelopes to be postmarked with the trip's date.

The service being rendered by the *Westcott* is not something new. It goes back to 1895, the year that the J. W. Westcott Company first contracted with the U.S. Post Office Department to provide nautical mail service. In those days, a different delivery system was used. A man in a rowboat was towed into the path of an oncoming ship. Using his oars, he would maneuver close enough to the vessel to throw a line across. Then he would hitch a mail pouch to the line and it would be pulled aboard. An 1896 issue of *Harper's Weekly* described the feat as being "exceedingly dangerous."

Although the *Westcott*'s powerful diesel engines enable the craft to make its own deliveries, there are still some hazards. Foggy days are especially trying. Ships anchor until the fog begins to lift and then come down the river together like a ghost fleet. The *Westcott* chases up and down, back and forth, trying to catch as many ships as possible.

In his twenty-four years at the helm of the *Westcott,* Captain Adamek has never collided with another vessel. His record isn't unblemished, however. About twice a year mail falls into the river.

"For dependability," says Bernard Verreau, Assistant Director of Operations for Transit Mails of the Detroit Post Office, "the *Westcott* has a better record than the airlines. Service is curtailed only a couple of times a year, and then it's only for part of the day."

The crew of the *Westcott* delivers postage-due letters and counts on the addressee's honesty to put the money in the pail on the return trip. The crew once found a $5 bill in the pail along with a note of thanks after delivering a postage-due letter. The letter was from a sailor's girl and had helped to patch up a lovers' quarrel.

Steamer officers and crew members have many other reasons to be grateful

The Westcott *is dwarfed by a huge freighter*
U.S. POSTAL SERVICE

Under way on the Detroit River
U.S. POSTAL SERVICE

to the *Westcott.* Detroit River Station, home of the mail boat, once radioed the captain of a river steamer to tell him that a registered parcel was waiting for him. "Deliver it as soon as possible," the captain radioed back.

The *Westcott* took the package on its next trip. The captain was waiting on deck as the boat drew up. He reached into the pail, drew out the package, examined it, then smiled and saluted in the direction of the *Westcott.* The package contained the captain's new dentures.

Once in a while the crew of the *Westcott* is involved in an emergency situation. One day while the boat was making its nautical rounds, a crew member saw a woman fall from the Ambassador Bridge, the span over the Detroit River that links Detroit and Windsor, Canada. Some crew members hauled the woman out of the water

South of Detroit, less than 100 miles from the *Westcott*'s duty station, the waters of Lake Erie have served to isolate other of the Postal Service's customers. These are the residents of Kelleys Island and the Bass Islands, a cluster of four small, heavily wooded dots of land just north of Sandusky, Ohio.

To get mail to the several hundred people who populate these islands, the Postal Service relies on the *Tin Goose*, a Ford tri-engined aircraft that dates to 1929. It looks about as much like one of today's big and powerful jets as Columbus' *Santa Maria* might have resembled the *Queen Elizabeth II*.

One of the *Tin Goose*'s three propeller-equipped engines is mounted at

Away goes the mail pail

and gave her artificial respiration. Captain Adamek radioed for an ambulance to meet the boat. The woman was the only person ever to survive a fall from the Ambassador Bridge.

There's a footnote to the incident. A few days after the rescue, Captain Adamek received a call from U.S. Customs officials. They queried him about smuggling an alien across the border from Canada. "After I heard that," the captain declared, "I decided I'd go back to picking up the mail, and *only* the mail."

At the wheel—Captain William Adamek

The Tin Goose *takes on its mail load*

A Ford emblem decorates the Tin Goose's *flank*

becoming a reality, the Ford plane was involved in many aviation "firsts." It was, for example, the plane that the intrepid Bernt Balchen piloted to the South Pole in November, 1929, one of his many pioneering efforts.

The *Tin Goose* has been the connecting link between the islands and the northern Ohio shore for more than forty years. Why use an airplane? The distance is short, only nine and one half miles to the nearest of the islands. Why not make deliveries by boat? It is because boats aren't able to operate in the winter months. Beginning about the middle of November, fierce winds blow. Later in the winter the lake becomes sheeted with ice and stays that way for weeks.

But why an airplane that's more than forty years old? Why not a mod-

the plane's nose; the other two are fixed beneath the big wing, one on each side. The plane is called the *Tin Goose* because it dates to a time before airplanes were fabricated of aluminum. Its body is made of sheets of fluted tin that have been riveted in place.

To watch the *Tin Goose* lumber down the runway and then ease into the air is like taking a glimpse into aviation's deep past. Dating to the era when commercial flying was only just

40

Prop-equipped engines represent a bygone era in aviation history

ern plane? "The old Ford is perfect for the conditions we encounter," says Ralph Dietrick, president of Island Airlines and owner of the *Tin Goose*. "The only paved airstrip we have is on South Bass. On the other islands [North Bass, Middle Bass, and Kelleys Island], we have to put down on and take off from dirt strips.

"In the spring, there's deep mud; in the winter, heavy snow. But the *Tin Goose*'s big wheels go right through. A modern plane would get stuck. And the *Tin Goose* also has a rear wheel, which helps.

"Another thing: the *Tin Goose* gets up in the air quickly, even when we've got a heavy load. This is important, because the runways are short."

The *Tin Goose* departs from Port Clinton on the mainland each morning and completes its four-island delivery run in less than an hour. During the summer months, when many vacationists populate the islands, the *Tin Goose* also makes an afternoon delivery.

Dietrick, who purchased the airline and its plane in 1953, has since bought up several other tri-motored Ford airplanes and whatever engines he has been able to find. He uses their parts to keep the *Tin Goose* running. Dietrick says that he has sufficient parts to keep the *Tin Goose* flying until the 1980's. Its last stop will surely be a museum.

When it comes to unusual methods of delivering the mail, no report would be complete without mention of difficulties postal authorities face in getting letters and packages into the Havasupai Indian village of Supai, a virtually hidden village whose small homes and stores are to be found at the very bottom of the Havasu Canyon, 2,400 feet beneath the South Rim of the Grand Canyon. It is one of the most sequestered spots in America.

Historians and archaeologists say that the Havasupai homelands were settled some eight hundred years ago. The Federal Government declared the area to be a reservation in 1880.

The towering sandstone walls have helped the Indians preserve their cultural identity and many of their customs, but at the same time they have prevented many of civilization's comforts and conveniences from reaching them. There are no newspapers, no

Loading mail for the trek to Supai
U.S. POSTAL SERVICE

Entering Supai

Postmistress Hanna sorts and distributes letters and packages

U.S. POSTAL SERVICE

television. None of the fifty homes that make up Supai has electricity.

There are movies, however. Each week a film from the world "up on top" makes its descent into the village. It is shown at the village recreation center. Indian audiences have a clearcut preference as to what they want to see—they like Westerns.

Mail is probably more important to the 300 inhabitants of Supai than it is to any other group of Americans anywhere. It is the villagers' one vital communications link with the world outside.

The only practical way of getting the mail to Supai is on the back of a mule. Three times a week, sacks of letters and packages from the post office in Kingman, Arizona, are delivered by pickup truck to the rim of the canyon where a mule train is waiting. After the sacks are loaded, the packers mount their horses and the arduous downward trek begins. The route covers eight tortuous miles of switchbacks, hogbacks, and winding trails.

Once the mule train reaches the canyon floor, it's a short trip to the Supai Post Office, a small wood-frame building that postmistress Virginia Hanna shares with a clinic operated by the Public Health Service. She promptly distributes the mail to waiting customers.

A small, audacious boat, a forty-year-old airplane, a pack of sure-legged mules—all these makes one wonder. Surely, somewhere the pony express is still operating.

5

ON A LAYER OF AIR

You CAN PUT a 25-ton load aboard, and then drive it with ease over rolling terrain, swamps, ice, mud, snow, water, or a concrete highway. It goes forward, backward, or to either side.

You can hover it like a helicopter. Set it down on a lake and it will float like a raft. It can climb a 20-percent grade, whisk from land to water and back again, zip over water at 45 miles an hour and over land at very close to that speed.

It's the Voyageur, a self-propelled cargo deck that travels on a cushion of air. Two such ships began operation in the oilfields of the Canadian Arctic in 1973, and they quickly proved to be of enormous value in transporting heavy equipment and a variety of resupply missions.

Unlike an automobile, a train, or a boat, the Voyageur has no physical contact with the surface over which it operates. Unlike an airplane or a helicopter, it is unable to rise above the surface more than a few feet. It represents the only really unique form of

transportation developed in the past fifty years.

The Voyageur is powered by a pair of gas turbine engines, each capable of delivering 1,300 horsepower. A T-shaped gear system transmits power from each engine to a big lift fan. It is these fans that create the pressure bubble of air on which the Voyageur rides.

A pair of propellers mounted verti-

The Voyageur *on a test run*
BELL AEROSPACE CO. DIVISION OF TEXTRON CANADA LTD.

44

cally at the rear of the vehicle provide forward thrust. Speed is regulated by simply adjusting propeller pitch. The propellers also help in turning, but for high-speed turns the vehicle relies on two aerodynamic rudders mounted at the stern. Each of these consists of a hinged metal plate which, when turned to the right or left, causes the craft to change direction.

The Voyageur is operated from a raised cabin placed toward the after end of the deck that looks something like a tugboat's elevated pilothouse. It takes two men to operate the Voyageur—a pilot and a radar specialist. The cabin contains additional seating for four passengers. But basically the Voyageur is a cargo carrier. One look at its big open deck is proof of that. It is 36′ × 64′, enough space to play a game of tennis.

When the Voyageur was put to work in the Arctic, it faced a difficult test. The terrain there is such that most vehicles are virtually helpless.

Strictly speaking, the Arctic refers to the geographical area extending from the North Pole to the northern timberline. For centuries it was believed that the region was a perpetually frozen, completely barren place. Scientists know differently today. Except for Greenland, 90 percent of all Arctic regions, in the summer months, at least, have no snow or ice.

What they do have is tundra, a word used to describe low-lying, swampy areas that border the Arctic Ocean, not only in North America but in

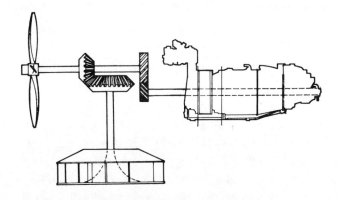

A drive shaft leading from the Voyageur's *gas turbine engines supplies power to both the lift fan and propeller by means of a T-shaped gear system*

northern Europe and in Siberia. The ground remains frozen to great depths all year round, but in the Arctic summer a few feet of the surface thaws. Hundreds of different kinds of plants grow in this region, mostly mosses, lichens, and stunted shrubs.

Besides the tundra, there is the Arctic Ocean itself, a constantly shifting ice cover that stretches for millions of square miles. It is interlaced with an ever-changing network of ice fields, pressure ridges, and vast expanses of open water.

No one knows for certain what mineral deposits lie beneath the Arctic tundra. But recent explorations have indicated that they include vast resources of metallic ores and great reservoirs of coal—low-sulfur coal, the type of coal that the pollution-conscious United States is seeking. There is evidence that important amounts of gold are to be found on the northern continental shelf on Norton Sound off the coast of Nome.

All these treasures may prove insignificant compared to the Arctic oil and gas riches. Discoveries in Alaska and Canada in recent years have touched off an "oil rush." Scores of rigs are drilling along the middle section of Alaska's North Slope, which stretches approximately five hundred miles west from the Canadian border between the Brooks Range and the Arctic Ocean. Activity is also being stepped up on Canada's Mackenzie basin and on Arctic islands, north of the 60th parallel.

Arctic transportation is frequently air transportation, with big planes such as the C-130 Hercules, the Boeing-727 and -737, and even the old Douglas DC-3 serving remote airstrips. But Arctic air transport has its failings. Landing strips in most areas, most of them hurriedly constructed and poorly maintained, are accessible only during certain months of the year. And even when an aircraft is able to set down and unload, the cargo it delivers must then be surface-transported to its final destination.

Helicopters have provided valuable service in the Arctic, but they also have some drawbacks—their range is limited, they can operate only when weather conditions permit, and they are restricted as to the amount of payload they can carry.

Big-tracked vehicles have been able to haul cargo over the tundra during periods of thaw. But they present another problem. Environmentalists have

protested the use of such vehicles because they mar the terrain, their heavy steel tracks scarring everything they come in contact with. As a result, tracked vehicles have been banned from Arctic Canada and Alaska's North Slope during the summer months, when the region is most susceptible to ecological damage.

Conventional modes of surface transport are practically nonexistent. Most of the roads have been constructed of riverbed gravel and are passable only during the winter months when the ground is frozen solid. It is unthinkable to travel over one during a period of thaw.

Railroads? The amount of track that has been laid is insignificant.

Rivers are shallow, winding, and strewn with boulders. They are not navigable by anything bigger than a canoe, and this in the summer only. All rivers are ice-clogged during the winter months.

Frozen terrain and snow are no problem for the Voyageur

BELL AEROSPACE CO. DIVISION OF TEXTRON CANADA LTD.

The ACT-100, the largest air-cushion vessel in the world

ARCTIC ENGINEERS AND CONSTRUCTORS

Snowmobiles? They are able to transport only puny loads. Dog teams and sleds? They are of another era and play only the smallest of roles today.

The difficulties posed by Arctic climate and terrain scarcely affect the Voyageur. It can operate the year round over land, water, ice, or snow, and also over what is referred to as marginal terrain—marshland, scrubland, and tundra. And it does no harm to the environment. Indeed, the Voyageur is the only surface vehicle permitted to operate over the tundra of Alaska's North Slope during the May-to-October period of thaw.

Not only has the Voyageur demonstrated its ability to negotiate Arctic tundra, it has also operated over heretofore unnavigable waterways. One Voyageur made the 80-mile trip from Sagwon Airport to Prudhoe Bay by means of the wild Sagavanirktok River, a waterway no boat had ever

navigated. The trip took only two hours.

Another went from Yellowknife on the Great Slave Lake, up the Mackenzie River, and west along the Arctic coast to Prudhoe Bay. This voyage and others similar provided very helpful findings on the nature of ice formations, information that will be valuable to future expeditions.

Soon the Voyageur may have company, for a second vehicle of this type is being readied for Arctic use. This craft is bigger; indeed, it is the biggest air-cushion vehicle ever built. Its open deck measures 57' × 75', almost enough space for two tennis courts side by side.

But this vehicle, which was successfully tested across stretches of the prairies of Alberta in 1971, is not self-propelled. After it has lifted itself off the ground, it must be towed, just the way a barge is towed downriver by a small boat. In this case a tractorlike

A section of the skirt system of the Voyageur. *Air is introduced to and emitted from triangular "fingers"*

BELL AEROSPACE CO. DIVISION OF TEXTRON CANADA LTD.

47

vehicle does the towing. The rig doesn't travel very fast—only about 6 miles an hour.

Plans are to use the transporter for the delivery of equipment, supplies, and prefabricated structures. It can carry a payload about four times that of the Voyageur, or 100 tons. The transporter can also serve as a combination work platform and housing site, able to accommodate 60 men.

No one claims that air-cushion vehicles are going to solve all the problems of Arctic transportation. But they are solving some of them. In years to come, they are likely to take on a real workhorse role.

The air-cushion vehicle, sometimes called a hovercraft, hydroskimmer, or surface-effect ship, was the invention of a mustachioed British electronics engineer and part-time boat builder named Sydney Cockerell. In 1948, after he had opened a small boat rental agency, Cockerell became intrigued by the problem of wave resistance. "Why can't boats go any faster?" was the question he kept asking himself. He knew that if he could get some kind of lubricant between a boat's hull and the water, he could reduce friction and increase the craft's speed.

Grease, machine oil, and graphite are the best-known lubricants. Cockerell was to try an unusual one: air. He realized that air was 815 times less dense than water. The next step was to devise a way of introducing a continuous flow of air between the boat's hull and the water's surface.

Cockerell began experimenting with a pair of coffee cans, one slightly larger than the other. He nested the small one into the big one. Then, using his wife's hair dryer, he blew a steady stream of air into the slim opening between the two cans. "I found that the air followed the 'predicted' path," he said, "and that there *was* a gain in lift. It was very exciting!"

By 1953, Cockerell had developed a small working model of an air-cushion vehicle. He then encountered unexpected difficulties. When he took the idea to a shipbuilder and tried to sell it, he was told, "That's no ship. It flies. Take it to an aircraft company."

When he approached any aircraft firm, he was invariably told, "That's no airplane. Go and see a shipbuilder."

But Cockerell continued his development work and, in 1957, began construction of an experimental vehicle, known as the SR.N1. Cockerell's daring flight across the English Channel in the SR.N1 on July 25, 1959, made history.

By present-day standards, the SR.N1 was a primitive machine. With its sharp-pointed bow and cases of equipment stacked all around, it looked like an overladen fishing boat, except for a big open-mouthed funnel that had been installed amidships. Air to support the vehicle was drawn in through the funnel.

At 3:30 A.M. on the morning of July 25, pilot Peter Lamb saw that the sea was flat and calm. After a conference between Lamb, Cockerell, and de-

Here the Voyageur *serves as a commuter's ferryboat*

BELL AEROSPACE CO. DIVISION OF TEXTRON CANADA LTD.

signer Richard Stanton-Jones, it was decided to make the attempt. Lamb revved up the engine and sent the ungainly-looking craft skimming over the still water of Calais harbor. Their destination, Dover, England, was about 25 miles away.

About halfway across, the white cliffs of Dover, tinged a soft pink by the morning sun, became visible. The wind began to build in intensity and the waves grew treacherous. Salt spray showered Lamb and his passengers continuously, making them wet and cold and causing their eyes to smart. But before long they were in the shelter of the cliffs, protected from the wind.

Lamb brought the craft into the Dover harbor smartly, at a speed of 25 knots. Those watching marveled that there was no wave action from the strange craft. At 6:58 A.M., Lamb ran the SR.N1 up onto a beach, and the historic trip was over. Looking back in later years, Cockerell observed, "We were lucky to get away with it."

More development work followed the success of the SR.N1. By the late 1960's, the British Hovercraft Corporation was turning out commercial models that were used to ferry passengers and autos across the English Channel. Four ships were in cross-Channel operation by 1970, each capable of carrying 250 passengers and 30 automobiles.

Stepping aboard one of these ships is something like going aboard a modern commercial jet plane. There's an

49

aircraft-style cabin with aircraft-style seating. But there are no safety belts, and passengers are permitted to smoke before "takeoff."

When the pilot starts the four giant marine engines, each of which drives a 4-bladed propeller and a big lift fan, the craft rises gently to cruising level— about 7 feet. Then, by increasing the bite of the propellers, the pilot eases the vehicle forward and out of Dover harbor. Inside the cabin, you quickly get used to the steady throb of the engines; the noise level is less than that of a conventional propeller aircraft. Once outside the harbor, the pilot increases speed to 50 knots.

While there is no sideways roll, the ship does pitch forward and backward, especially if the sea happens to be choppy. The trip has been described as being about as rough as riding a horse at a trot. Seasickness is not unknown. No one goes out on the deck; after all, there is a 50-knot gale blowing out there.

Within 35 minutes after their departure from Dover, the passengers step down the airline-type stairs onto the French beach at Boulogne. The steam ferry, the conventional means of crossing from England to France, takes two hours. The one-way fare for a small car with two passengers is $19 by hovercraft, about a third more than the trip costs by steamer.

There's nothing experimental about these ships. They make 12 Channel crossings a day, toting as much as 50 tons each time. As an official for the

British Hovercraft Corporation points out, "William the Conquerer needed 700 ships to bring 10,000 invaders from France in two days. In that much time we could have moved them all with *one* of our new model ships."

Don't confuse hovercraft of this type with the hydrofoil. The hydrofoil is a boat with underwater "wings," a set of bladelike structures that jut out from each side of the hull. When the craft starts forward, the motion of the water flowing over the blades has the same effect as air rushing over an airplane's wing, and acts to lift the boat out of the water. With the water's friction sharply reduced, the boat is able to travel at higher speeds than conventional overwater craft.

There's a much different operating principle involved in the air-cushion vehicles turned out by the British Hovercraft Corporation and by Bell Aerospace Canada, the firm that manufactures the Voyageur. These latter vehicles depend on a fan (or fans), which sucks in air through the top of the vehicle, creating a bubble of air beneath the drum-shaped hull. When the air pressure is sufficient, the craft lifts from the surface.

This basic principle has been modified somewhat. Instead of simply filling the chamber beneath the hull with air and allowing it to escape, it is more efficient to release the air in a continuous stream from around the periphery of the hull bottom. This peripheral jet system produces much greater upward pressure, much greater lift.

50

The use of flexible skirts around the periphery of the hull bottom was a second important modification. Made of tough, rubberized nylon, the skirts hang from both the inner and outer edges of the peripheral air duct. Actually, the skirts are an extension of the duct, and as such they serve to increase the height at which the vehicle travels.

Should the vehicle strike a boulder, tree stump, or wave, the skirt "gives," then returns to its normal position. There is only a momentary interruption in the flow of air. Passengers aren't even likely to notice.

The Voyageur is equipped with what is known as a bag skirt. It looks like a big tube fixed to the outer periphery of the hull bottom. Into the bottom of the skirt have been fitted hundreds of small triangular-shaped "fingers." Air supplied to the skirt from intake fans is emitted through openings in the fingers (diagram, p. 47).

By mid-1972, approximately one hundred air-cushion vehicles had been built and were being used in a variety of tasks throughout the world. The British maintain leadership in the production of these craft, but other nations are beginning to challenge, Canada, the United States, France, and Japan among them.

Bell Aerospace Canada forecasts a role for the Voyageur in helping to solve the mass transit problems that big cities are experiencing. Most cities, the company points out, evolved during a period when water transportation was dominant, and so are located on a seacoast, major river, or are part of a lake waterway system.

"These waterways are now neglected," says a company spokesman. "In fact, they often form a natural barrier to city transportation, with cars, trucks, and other vehicles having to be funneled into bridges or tunnels."

One way to untangle things would be to use bus transportation and the Voyageur in combination. A commuter would board a bus near his home, and it would carry him to a Voyageur terminal located at an approach point to the inner city. This bus and several others would be driven aboard the Voyageur, which would then carry the commuters over an existing waterway to a downtown terminal. In this way, the commuters would avoid the traffic-clogged streets of the inner city.

Besides cutting down on their travel time, it would save them money too. The system also offers convenience, for the passengers would never have to change from one mode of transportation to another. Once a commuter had settled down in his bus seat, he would remain there until he reached his destination.

Many nations of the world are considering air-cushion vehicles for military purposes. When British forces participated in patrols and landings during the North Atlantic Treaty Organization's operations in Norway in 1972, they used hovercraft for a variety of jobs. Some patrolled fjords seeking "hostile" ships. Others took landing parties ashore to attack "enemy" outposts. United States military observers were impressed by the speed and versatility of the hovercrafts.

One British air-cushion vehicle is known as the VT-1. It may be the forerunner of the type of hovercraft that one day will be in widespread use by the navies of the world. A 100-ton vessel with a speed of 46 knots, the VT-1 is frequently used as a coastal patrol vessel. It is armed with four antiship missile launchers and a twin-barreled 35mm. cannon for antiaircraft and antisubmarine operations. Because it needs no deepwater port or anchorage, the VT-1 is expected to be especially valuable to small nations.

United States military experts, who refer to air-cushion vehicles as surface-effect ships, are well beyond the planning stage in vehicle technology. The Navy is expected to have a 2,200-ton air-cushion vehicle operating with the fleet by the end of 1976. On the drawing boards are plans for a 10,000-ton air-cushion vehicle that would be equipped with landing platforms for helicopters and STOL (Short-Take-Off-and-Landing) aircraft.

The Navy would use air-cushion vehicles in antisubmarine operations and in defending surface ships from air attack. Ships utilizing the air-cushion principle, the Navy believes, would be extremely difficult targets for guided missiles and would be safe from torpedo attack. Their speed would be such that they would simply outrace any torpedo.

52

The Navy tests an air-cushion vehicle
U.S. NAVY

Some naval experts say that if all goes as planned, surface ships as they are known today will be on the verge of being obsolete by the mid-1980's. This applies not only to naval vessels but to merchant ships as well. Surface-effect ships designed as cargo carriers could speed from New York to northern Europe and back in about three days, considerably less than half the time the trip now takes.

What's exciting about air-cushion vehicles is that so many developments have taken place in such a short span of time. It was only about two decades ago that Sydney—now Sir Sydney—Cockerell began experimenting with coffee cans and his wife's hair dryer. As one observer has put it, "It's as if the Model T Ford were running a decade after the invention of the wheel."

Air-cushion vehicles are not going to render the wheel obsolete or cause passengers to abandon the airplane or transatlantic steamship travel. But they have proven their value in a variety of commercial applications, and no one denies that they have a bright future.

6

MODERN NOAHS

G IRAFFES WALK beside you. Lions roam free. Tigers pace and stalk. There are birds of every color and description in the drive-through zoo, the newest trend in the exhibition of wild animals. From the safety of your automobile (with windows rolled up, of course), you have close-up views of animals from the four corners of the earth, everything from an aoudad to a zebra.

While Europe has had drive-through zoos for some time, it wasn't until 1967 that the first one was opened in the United States. Located in West Palm Beach, Florida, and known as Lion Country Safari, it covers 647 acres and features over 100 lions, a zebra herd, elephants, giraffes, and rhinos. There are now four such parks in operation in the United States.

Jungle Habitat in West Milford, New Jersey, opened in 1972. Visitors drive over a 4-mile road which winds through its 1,000 acres. Peering through car windows, the visitor can see leopards, zebras, dromedary camels, tigers, lions—some 1,500 wild ani-

Drive-through zoos are the newest concept in the exhibition of wild animals
JUNGLE HABITAT

mals in all. Dozens of other drive-through zoos are being planned. By the end of the decade, it will be difficult to find an American boy or girl who doesn't know what it is like to go on safari.

Because the "industry" of the drive-through zoo is booming, so is the business of supplying wild animal stock. Almost all zoo animals exhibited in the United States, either in the drive-through zoos or in the more familiar type of zoos, are purchased from deal-

53

ers, men who specialize in capturing the animals (or in having them captured) and then arrange for their transportation to the United States. There are about a dozen well-known and reputable dealers who serve American zoos.

Zoo directors receive dealer price lists in the mail almost every day. With a single telephone call, a zoo official can order a Siberian tiger, a European brown bear, giraffes, elephants, zebras —almost anything. Jungle Habitat recently purchased an entire herd of zebras, 32 animals in all, from International Animal Exchange, the largest of the companies supplying zoo animals. The zebra herd traveled in a body from Africa to New York aboard a chartered jet, and now roam the "plains" of New Jersey together.

Big animals, such as rhinoceroses or anything larger, usually travel to the United States by freighter. Smaller animals go by air. But no matter what type of transportation is involved, dealing in zoo animals is never simple.

Animals have to be protected from injury during shipment, which usually means that special crates have to be built. Animals have to be fed the right food en route. They have to be pro-

Big animals travel by ship

Smaller animals, like the cheetah, go by air

tected from extremes in temperature. They have to be watched over for symptoms of sickness and disease. "It's a lot easier to haul expensive color television sets or rare French wine," says an airline official, "than it is to carry a crateful of penguins or some antelope. You don't just ship animals. You have to baby-sit with them."

The idea of capturing and exhibiting wild animals is very old, dating to the earliest of times. Kings and nobles put caged animals on display to indicate that their authority extended to every creature. With a chained tiger at his feet, a reigning monarch graphically demonstrated his powerfulness, his supremacy.

Ancient kings frequently sent gifts of exotic animals to one another in an expression of regard and friendship. King Hiram of Tyre, says the Bible, sent to his ally, King Solomon of Judah, tribute that included both pre-

cious metals and animals. "Once every three years," states I Kings 10:22, "the fleet of ships of Tarshish used to come bringing gold, silver, ivory, apes, and peacocks."

There are any number of modern examples of this practice, but the animals usually travel by air rather than by ship. Premier Nikita Khrushchev of the Soviet Union once sent a bear cub to Great Britain's Princess Anne. The offspring of gift lions donated by Ethiopian emperor Haile Selassie are to be found in zoos throughout the world.

Premier Chou En-lai presented President Nixon with a pair of rare giant pandas as a gift from the people of China to "the people of the United States" during Nixon's visit to China in 1972. The pandas now reside in the National Zoological Park in Washington, D.C.

Gift panda frolics in the National Zoo, Washington, D. C.

The first zoos of which there is historical evidence are those depicted on the walls of Egyptian tombs. Wild goats, gazelles, and great-horned eryxes, a type of antelope now almost extinct, are represented as zoo animals. Archaeologists say that these tomb paintings date to 2500 B.C. The ancient Chinese, too, kept wild animals, exhibiting them in what were called "gardens of intelligence."

Aristotle, the great Greek philosopher who lived from 384 to 322 B.C., found such an enormous variety of birds and animals in the Greek zoo that he was able to write his *History of Animals,* the first scientific work in the field of zoology. In it he described more than 300 individual species.

The imperial city of Rome maintained a huge zoo, one that was well stocked with the biggest and fiercest animals that could be found. They were mostly used in the arenas. In addition, Rome had a number of private zoos, established and maintained by private citizens. When the Roman scholar, Pliny the Elder, wrote his *Natural History* in the first century, an encyclopedia of natural history, one volume was devoted to zoology and was based upon his observation of the many and varied Roman zoo animals.

Emperor Charlemagne, who reigned during the eighth century as king of the Franks, maintained three zoos. William the Conquerer, king of England from 1066–1087, though he lacked both wealth and power, still managed to have a royal zoo. It was

56

Zoos have been places of entertainment for over a century. This is a scene in the London Zoo in 1871

the forerunner of the deer parks that were to become popular among England's landed gentry.

One thing that makes the early zoos so remarkable is the fact that so few mechanical aids existed for capturing and transporting animals. Sailing vessels were one method. For overland travel, cages were hoisted by pulley and capstan onto heavy wagons, which sometimes were pulled by elephants.

The oldest zoo in continuous operation is the Vienna zoo, opened in 1765. The first zoo planned in the United States was the Philadelphia Zoological

Garden, but the Civil War struck before it could begin operation. Credit for being the oldest zoo in the United States goes to the Central Park Zoo in New York City, established in 1864. Still in operation, it offers visitors a collection of about one hundred animals representing fifty different species. The next oldest zoos in the United States are Buffalo's Zoological Gardens and Chicago's Lincoln Park Zoological Gardens.

Today the United States has about four hundred collections of animals, of which about fifty are major zoos. There is a growing trend toward charging admissions, but the majority of American zoos are free.

Although the concept of exhibiting animals dates to ancient times, the history of animal dealers is brief, covering not much more than a century. The first animal dealers were men who lived or worked near city docks, where shipmasters and sailors occasionally offered rare birds and animals for sale. So it was with Claas Hagenbeck, one of the first animal dealers history has made note of. A fish dealer in Hamburg, Germany, Hagenbeck was well known and well liked by German sailors, and they often gave him exotic animals. Eventually, Hagenbeck opened a small zoo in Hamburg. His collection included six pup seals, some hyenas, and a polar bear.

An elephant being hoisted from an animal ship seventy years ago

ST. NICHOLAS MAGAZINE, FEB. 1904

The elder Hagenbeck remained a fish dealer, but his son, Karl, devoted himself exclusively to the capture and exhibit of wild animals, and in time became one of the most noted of all dealers. Not only did he supply zoos and circuses with animals from every part of the world, but he took an interest in animal-training methods. Whips and white-hot irons were frequently used in training animals to become performers. Hagenbeck believed that such inhumane treatment was unnecessary. In 1889 he exhibited three lions who had been broken to harness and taught to pull a chariot without having been whipped or burned. Hagenbeck's success helped to change training methods for all time.

Hagenbeck established a zoo in the town of Stellingen, near Hamburg, in 1907. He was the first to exhibit animals in the open, with wide moats and not bars separating the animals and visitors. This method of exhibition is seen frequently today. The Hagenbeck zoo was badly damaged by bombing during World War II, but after the war it was rebuilt by Karl's grandson, Karl-Heinrich Hagenbeck.

Until fairly recent times, most large American zoos sent out their own collecting expeditions. They were adventures for all concerned. One was the Smithsonian-Chrysler Expedition, which sailed from New York in the spring of 1926. The party, headed by Dr. William Mann, director of the National Zoological Park in Washington, D.C., included scientists, veterinarians, game-handlers, and newsreel cameramen. Equipment and supplies were provided by the Marine Corps, medicines by a Washington hospital.

After arrival in East Africa, the expedition moved inland and established headquarters at Dodoma in what is now central Tanzania. There they hired interpreters and local hunters. After four months of hunting, trapping, and collecting, the expedition returned to the United States in triumph, bringing giraffes, gnus, impalas, koodoos, elands, leopards, hyenas, foxes, ratels, and countless other prizes.

Those days have gone the way of the trolley car. Zoo officials today are concerned with caring for the animals, feeding them properly, exhibiting them imaginatively, and, more and more, with the development of sound conservation practices. They leave the matter of capturing and transporting the animals to specialists, to animal dealers.

Most of the animals that wind up in American zoos today are taken from the wild and transported to the United States by the International Animal Exchange, a firm with headquarters in Ferndale, Michigan. The company was founded by Don Hunt, who became interested in animals as a boy of eleven when he began working in a Detroit pet shop. He eventually saved enough money to buy the store. Little by little, he began to import animals—first, guinea pigs for a drug manufacturer, then a playful chimpanzee who became a local television star, then others.

Today, Hunt lives most of the year at his game ranch on the slopes of Mount Kenya. In one recent year, Hunt supplied a cheetah for a zoo in Brookfield, Illinois; another cheetah for the Cleveland zoo, a giraffe for the Detroit zoo, a number of Thomson's gazelles for the Oklahoma zoo, a rhinoceros for the Toledo zoo, and one for the Cincinnati zoo. For a new zoo in Brownsville, Texas, Hunt agreed to supply $1.5 million in animals, a 2-year project.

Obviously, the first step is to capture the animal. Many methods are used. Take the case of a herd of 18 rhinos that arrived not long ago at the San Diego Wild Animal Farm. They came from the Umfolzi Game Reserve in South Africa, not far from Durban on the southeast coast.

After skilled horsemen had found the rhino herd, the animals were darted one by one with a tranquilizing drug fired from a rifle. As the rhinos lay unconscious, crates were unloaded from trucks and one was placed near each animal. An antidote was then injected into each rhino that, after a few minutes, permitted him to stand and walk into the crate.

Although tranquilizer darts are helpful in subduing some animals, they can be dangerous to others. An incorrect dosage of the drug might be fatal.

Zebras and giraffes are captured from a jeep or a Land Rover. The hunters rig the vehicle with long poles. Each pole is fitted with a running noose at one end. The hunters journey

After being darted with a tranquilizer, the rhino is given an antidote intravenously. He can then be coaxed into his crate

SAN DIEGO ZOO

59

out across the veldt in search of their quarry. When a zebra herd is sighted, the hunters pursue one of the animals and use the outstretched pole to loop the rope around the animal's neck. The vehicle is gently braked to a stop, so as not to injure the prize.

For trapping a Bengal tiger, natives dig a deep pit and build a 6-foot-high fence around its perimeter. A buffalo calf is placed in the bottom of the pit. Lured by the scent of the calf, the tiger leaps over the fence, landing at the bottom of the pit.

As the tiger devours the calf, natives build a cover over the top of the pit, but leave a tiger-size opening in the center. Now the natives bring baskets of dirt and empty them into the pit. As the pit fills, the tiger gets closer and closer to the opening at the top.

When the tiger is within a short leap of the pit opening, a stout cage is brought up. An opening in the bottom of the cage is placed over the pit opening.

To get the tiger out of the now shallow pit and into the cage, the natives rely on a small and very agile dog, which they drop into the pit. The tiger springs for the dog, but the nimble animal escapes through the pit opening into the cage and on out the open end. The tiger, in his headlong pursuit of the dog, leaps out of the pit and into the cage, too, but before he can escape, a native slams shut the sliding door. Other natives quickly seal the opening in the cage bottom.

Lions and leopards are trapped in a somewhat similar fashion. Gorillas are netted. Small antelope are hunted at night. When the bright lights of a vehicle shine on them, the antelope stand motionless and can be captured easily.

"Catching the animal is the easy part," says Don Hunt. "It's after the capture that the work starts."

Many wild animals are put into pens to be "gentled"—pacified, made tame. In the case of zebras, handlers spend several days talking to the animals, so as to accustom them to the sound of the human voice. One trainer plays a tape recording of traffic sounds and airport noises for zebra herds, repeating the "selection" daily for weeks. During this time, the zebras are introduced to oats, corn, and soybeans, which will be staples in their zoo diet.

Boxing and crating animals for shipment is a special art. Not only does an animal's size determine the type of container in which he will travel, his temperament is also considered. Some animals don't mind being enclosed in a small space. They seem resigned to being captives and remain docile, but others snarl defiantly and never stop trying to escape.

Lions and tigers, despite their reputations, are not difficult to ship. "They're sulkers," says one animal transporter. "Cage them and keep them well fed, and they shouldn't give you any trouble."

The hoofed animals cause the most problems. Antelope, zebras, giraffes, and the like can thrash about and easily break a leg or otherwise injure them-

60

Hoofed animals, like this eland, are difficult to ship

openings at the bottom so that the container can be cleaned easily.

Penguins travel six to a crate, but they are isolated from one another by plywood walls that divide the container into six vertical compartments. Wire mesh covers the top of the crate.

When an ocean voyage is involved, dealers have to make arrangements with the steamship line to have the animals fed and the cages kept clean. Failure to be careful in setting down instructions can lead to tragedy. When a shipment of giraffes was sent from Mombasa, Kenya, to New York re-

selves. They have to be watched closely.

A zebra is shipped in a crate that gives freedom to his head and neck but keeps the rest of his body tightly confined. If the zebra were allowed the use of his legs, he would kick out wildly in an effort to gain his freedom. He might not get out but very likely he would injure a leg.

Polar bears are shipped in a cramped position. It seems cruel to confine the animal in a crate so small, but if the container were any larger, the bear would be able to exert his enormous strength and break free. Crates for animals like bears and zebras have slotted

A curious ostrich peers out from its shipping container

Most zoos assign veterinarians and handlers to care for animals being shipped by sea

cently, the wrong type of feed was put aboard. After the giraffes ate the food, a skin rash developed on their faces, causing an unbearable itch. The giraffes rubbed their heads against the crate slats with such ferocity that they scraped away big patches of skin. Before the voyage ended, the giraffes were dead. Many zoos, to guard against such happenings, assign trained handlers to travel with the animals and supervise their care and feeding.

Some jet flights are so swift that animals don't have to be fed while aboard. The most serious problems in shipping by air occur on the ground. Often animals must be transferred from one flight to another and may encounter a delay of several hours in between. Unless someone is on hand to meet the shipment, the animals may be made to withstand the rigors of the weather. They may have to go without food. At the biggest international airline terminals, humane societies operate animal shelters to guard against such occurrences.

Occasionally extreme heat causes difficulty. A shipment of penguins from the Antarctic once arrived at Kennedy Airport in New York during an August heat wave. After the birds were unloaded from their air-cooled aircraft, they faced a 6-hour wait before they were to be loaded aboard a second aircraft that was to take them to their final destination. Six hours of heat and humidity might have proved fatal, but quick-thinking airline employees saved the day. They located large blocks of ice and some electric fans and kept the birds bathed in cool breezes until their flight was ready for departure.

If you have ever traveled by air with a family pet, even across the country, you know that airlines have made pet travel a safe, simple matter. In the case of a small pet—a cat, household birds, or a small breed of dog such as a dachshund or a Pekingese—the airline will give you a free pet kennel, a rigid, ventilated container in which the pet rides. You simply stow the carton beneath your seat.

For a large animal (or an animal traveling alone), you must purchase a pet container. Airlines offer several sizes. The biggest costs about $30 and will hold a dog about the size of a German shepherd. Containers of this type are packed into a baggage compartment. Don't worry! It's heated and pressurized.

If you want to take your pet out of the country, check the regulations.

Chamroeun was the first elephant ever to be airlifted to the United States. Here his container is secured aboard the aircraft

Shots and papers may be required and a quarantine period may be necessary before you enter another country or before you bring your pet back into this country.

Once in a while public zoos receive animals as gifts. There was the case of an elephant, a battlefield veteran from war-torn Cambodia, that arrived at the Los Angeles zoo recently. Named Chamroeun, which means Prosperity, the elephant was captured by Cambodian soldiers from the Vietcong in 1971. President Lon Nol of Cambodia decided it would be a thoughtful gesture to present the elephant to Admiral John S. McCain, Jr., Commander in Chief of the United States Forces in the Pacific.

What does an admiral do with a 2,000-pound elephant? He donates it to a zoo, and in this case the Los Angeles zoo was the fortunate recipient.

Chamroeun was the first elephant ever shipped to the United States by air. Zoo officials went to Phnom Penh, Cambodia's capital, to supervise the construction of a stout metal and wood container to house Chamroeun in his 23-hour flight to Los Angeles. Despite an early morning Vietcong rocket attack that threatened to cancel the flight, Chamroeun made the Pacific crossing without incident. He was happily munching on bananas in his new home just a few hours after his arrival.

In most cases, animals do not go directly from their home countries to American zoos. The Animal Health

Division of the United States Department of Agriculture, in an effort to protect American agricultural animals from contagious diseases, requires that certain animals be kept isolated for a period of time to assure that they are free of disease. Special quarantine stations have been established for this purpose.

In the case of what the Department of Agriculture refers to as "wild ruminants," that is, hoofed, cud-chewing animals, such as antelope, zebras, deer, goats, sheep, and giraffes, quarantine regulations are especially rigid. This is because these animals are potential carriers of hoof-and-mouth disease, a highly contagious virus disease that could raise havoc with American beef and dairy herds, with sheep, or with other animals. While common in many countries, hoof-and-mouth disease is virtually unknown here.

When an antelope, for instance, is being brought from Kenya to the United States, the animal is first quarantined in Mombasa for 60 days and then released for shipping if disease-free. Upon arrival in the United States, the antelope is quarantined again, this time for 30 days. The Department of Agriculture maintains a quarantine station at Clifton, New Jersey, about twenty miles from New York City.

Surrounded by a high chain link fence, the station is made up of several-farm-type buildings that contain box stalls for the animals. The station is staffed by experienced veterinarians who observe the animals throughout their period of quarantine, draw blood samples from them for testing, and give each an identifying tattoo.

Other species of animals face similar regulations. Primates, an order of animals that includes apes and monkeys, and psittacine birds, that is, parrots and related birds, may carry diseases that humans can contract. The import of these animals is supervised by the Department of Health, Education and Welfare.

After being released from quarantine, the animals are put back into their crates and trucked to their zoo homes. "It takes a specialist to haul animals," says Harry Overbaugh, dean of animal transporters. "There can't be any fast starts or abrupt stops. You have to take your time on turns. If you cause an animal to fall, he can break a leg."

How much do zoos pay for animals? A giraffe costs about $7,000; a male antelope, $4,000; a lowland gorilla, up to $6,000; and a zebra, up to $2,500.

The lion, despite his renown as king of the jungle and his popularity among zoo visitors, is not expensive anymore. A zoo can purchase a lion for less than $2,000. The reason lions from abroad are not in sharp demand is that they breed easily in captivity. When a zoo purchases a lion from a dealer, it is usually only to replenish breeding stock.

One of the most costly of all zoo specimens is the okapi, an animal that is related to the giraffe and found in the

64

Congo region of Africa. The okapi carries a $10,000 price tag. A rhinoceros costs almost that much.

When a dealer imports a zoo animal, he encounters expenses at every turn. Take the case of a giraffe brought to the United States recently for the National Zoo in Washington by Frederik J. Zeehandelaar, one of the best-known suppliers of wild animals. The "jungle cost" of the giraffe was $1,000, the amount required to capture the animal and have it delivered to the collecting station at Arusha, Tanzania. As soon as Zeehandelaar had acquired the animal, he arranged life insurance protection for it, designating his firm as the beneficiary. The cost of the policy was $1,800. At Arusha, the giraffe was fed and crated, then trucked to Mombasa, 200 miles away. The cost: $300.

In Mombasa, the giraffe went into quarantine for 60 days. This cost Zeehandelaar $10 a day, or $600. The ocean voyage to New York, a $700 expense, came next, and then the giraffe was trucked to the quarantine station in Clifton. The trucker received $200. The giraffe's 30-day stay in Clifton added $300 to the bill. By the time the animal was ready for release from the quarantine station, Zeehandelaar had already incurred almost $5,000 in expenses. He still had to arrange to have the animal hauled to its ultimate destination and add in his own fee.

One of the biggest animal price tags of recent times belonged to a male takin, brought to the United States by Zeehandelaar in 1966 at the request of the Bronx Zoo. One of the rarest of living animals, indeed, a breed that is facing extinction, the takin is a goatlike mammal with backward-pointing horns and, in the case of the male, a golden coat. While the takin has many of the physical characteristics of cattle and appears as if he might be clumsy, he is agile and very fast.

The takin is native to the mountains of central Asia, specifically the high slopes of the Himalayas in a region that covers parts of both Burma and China. During the daylight hours, takin are seldom seen, concealing themselves in dense thickets of bamboo and rhododendron. Chinese and Burmese consider takin meat a delicacy, and through the centuries hunters have all but eliminated the species.

After obtaining a female takin in 1959, the Bronx Zoo began searching

The takin is one of the most expensive of all zoo animals

GEORGE SULLIVAN

65

for a male, hopeful that they could breed the animal, so helping to save the species. For this reason the zoo called upon Zeehandelaar.

The only available takin that Zeehandelaar knew of was a resident of a zoo in Rangoon, Burma. A male, less than a year old, he was just what the Bronx Zoo was seeking. But the price was high. The Rangoon Zoo wanted two giraffes and four zebras from Africa for their takin. Money didn't interest them.

Zeehandelaar had to purchase the giraffes and zebras and deliver them to the Rangoon Zoo before the officials would release the takin. He then had to arrange to ship the prize by air to Hamburg, Germany, where it was to be quarantined for 60 days, and then by freighter to New York, where the animal was again to be quarantined, at Clifton, for 30 days. What added to Zeehandelaar's problem was that his agreement with the Bronx Zoo specified that the purchase was limited "to this particular animal." Should the takin obtained in Rangoon have become ill and died, the Bronx Zoo would have accepted no substitute.

Despite all the problems, Zeehandelaar was able to deliver the takin safely to zoo officials. The effort involved trusted associates of Zeehandelaar in four continents—Europe, Africa, Asia, and North America.

A generation or so ago, an American wild animal hunter named Frank Buck attained widespread popularity. As an author, motion picture producer, wild animal authority, and proprietor of "Jungleland" at the New York World's Fair in 1939, Buck was as well known then as Joe Namath or Johnny Bench are today. One thing that helped to make Frank Buck popular was the catchphrase with which he came to be identified—"Bring 'em back alive!"

That slogan is out-of-date today. Zoo directors expect their newly delivered tenants to be free of disease, sound in limb, hale and fit in every way. Bringing " 'em" back merely alive isn't the idea anymore.

7

FOOD'S MAGIC CARPET

AMERICANS, it has been said, eat what they like. And what they like most are fresh foods—fruits and vegetables, meat, poultry, seafood.

New Yorkers and Chicagoans are used to strawberries for breakfast the year round. Fresh pineapples are shipped daily to Detroit, St. Louis, and San Francisco. Hawaiians seldom buy frozen chicken; they like it fresh.

People dining out tonight in Denver want Maine lobster. A couple in Atlanta orders king crab from Alaska and fresh sole from England.

Each one of these is a perishable, a word that the dictionary defines as a food product that is liable to spoilage or decay.

In the shipping of perishables, time is a critical factor. Each food product has its own "life-span." It must be transported from the field to the packing plant, and then shipped to a retail store or to a restaurant—all in a matter of hours.

Temperature is another important factor. Every perishable must be kept within a precise temperature range from the time that it is harvested until it reaches the customer.

Besides being sensitive to temperature, perishables are also sensitive to changes in humidity. There is a precise level of humidity for each.

How do growers and shippers solve the problems posed by time, temperature, and humidity? One answer is jet-age transportation. The other is containerization.

For decades, the air-cargo business was not much more than a stepchild of the passenger business, with most airlines merely tolerating anything they had to carry that didn't walk on two legs. They handled cargo shipments in much the same way that they handled passenger baggage, loading and unloading it piece by piece. Indeed, cargo shipments resembled passenger baggage in both size and weight and were stowed in the baggage compartments of passenger aircraft. Because these methods were so inefficient, the fees charged for air-cargo transport were high. Few shippers specified airfreight, as a result.

Two sizes of air-cargo containers
TRANS WORLD AIRLINES PHOTO

*Air-cargo containers are contoured to fit
snugly inside the cargo compartment*
LOCKHEED-CALIFORNIA CORP.

The picture began to change during
World War II. A few airlines, realizing
the market potential of air cargo,
bought surplus military planes or, in
some cases, converted commercial aircraft to carry cargo exclusively.

In the late 1950's, piston-powered
planes began to be replaced by turbo-
props, turbojets, and then by pure jets.
These aircraft, the pure jets in particular, were far larger than planes of the
past and offered increased space for
hauling cargo. In addition, the pur-

68

chase of these new, sophisticated aircraft put many airlines under severe
financial pressure. They were forced to
utilize each plane to the fullest.

Airlines began to mechanize their
methods of handling freight. It was
during this period that special containers to handle and carry freight
were introduced. Containers are now
available to shippers in many shapes
and sizes.

The type most frequently seen looks
like a big aluminum cube with one
edge lopped off. This odd form enables
the container to fit the structural shape
of the aircraft. A modern four-engined
jet has space for 30 such containers.

A grower shipping Hawaiian orchids
to Los Angeles, for example, loads the
container on his premises, then locks
and seals it, and has it delivered to
the air terminal. The container is not
opened until the customer receives it.

If it is perishables that are being
shipped, the container can be fitted
with a heating system or with refrigeration. Wire racks, bins, or sleeves
can also be installed.

The container protects the shipment
against sun, wind, and rain. And containers are virtually theft-proof. Expensive portable radios being shipped
from a manufacturer to points of distribution have always been tempting
targets for thieves, particularly when
the crates carry the manufacturer's
name and identifying label. Containers
conceal the nature of the goods.

The airfreight industry received another boost in the early 1970's when

the airlines began to introduce wide-bodied jets. There are three types: the Boeing-747, the McDonnell-Douglas DC-10, and the Lockheed-1011. All these aircraft are used in passenger service, but even with a full load of passengers and passenger baggage, each is capable of airlifting as much cargo as the smaller all-cargo jet freighters. In fact, each time an airline buys a wide-bodied jet, it is as though it bought about two thirds of a new jet freighter.

These new planes are not replacing the all-cargo jet. They are complementing them. The all-cargo jet flies at night. The wide-bodied jet usually flies during daylight hours, which are more convenient to the passengers it carries. This means that shippers have around-the-clock service at their disposal.

Paired containers are lined up for loading aboard a Lockheed-1011

The Boeing-747, the largest plane ever designed for commercial service, has three spacious cargo compartments, two for containerized cargo and one for bulk shipments. Loading the

Guide rails and rollers in the cargo-compartment deck permit even big loads to be stowed quickly

In the Boeing-747, the flight engineer's control panel reports on load's weight and balance

aircraft takes about as much time as loading the trunk of the family car. A power elevator raises the containers to the level of the cargo compartment. Guide rails and motor-driven rollers implanted in the deck of the cargo compartment permit handlers to slide each container quickly into place. Two men can load or unload a plane in less than half an hour.

The B-747 has one other important feature. When loading is completed, the flight engineer is able to obtain an accurate loading report on the plane's weight and how it is balanced. He simply consults a control panel at his flight station that is linked to electronic sensoring devices throughout the aircraft.

Window frames and side panels are the only evidence that this was once a passenger jet

Virtually all B-747's in service today carry both passengers and freight, but some models of the aircraft are "convertibles." The interior can be so altered that the aircraft becomes an all-freight carrier. It takes about twenty-four hours to make the conversion. The cabin is stripped bare of seats, carpeting, and other furnishings. It is also possible to fit the plane with a hinged nose to permit straight-on loading. When converted to all-freight use, a B-747 can transport a payload of more than 200,000 pounds at distances well beyond the transatlantic range.

Wide-bodied aircraft and the universal use of containers have already begun to make subtle changes in the way many products are marketed. It used to be that shirts in a department store were kept in expensive boxes on a shelf behind the counter. A clerk would go through the boxes to find the size and the color the customer wanted.

One seldom sees this system today. Shirts are arranged by size and color and displayed in the open. The customer does his own selecting. Shirt boxes have been eliminated because the shirts travel in containers from the manufacturer already arranged by size and color and ready to be placed on the counter.

It's the same with other types of clothing. Blouses and dresses move directly to retail outlets on hangers in containers.

Some fruits and vegetables that are on display almost daily in the nation's supermarkets were scarcely known to the American public a decade or so ago. Artichokes and avocados from California are two examples.

Or take the case of the papaya, a relatively new item on most produce counters outside Hawaii, where papayas are grown. A study prepared by a major airline in 1970 pointed to papayas as the commodity that could be utilized to fill in a slack period in the year-round shipment of Eastern-bound perishables. An education and promotion campaign helped to inform the American housewife about the merits of the papaya.

When growers used surface transport, they had to pick papayas before the fruit reached full maturity, allow-

This air freighter has a hinged nose to facilitate loading

BOEING

ing it to ripen in transit. The fruit never reached its peak of flavor as a result. Air transportation changed that. Now papayas are allowed to ripen fully before they are picked.

"Results have been encouraging," says an airline executive. "In terms of public acceptance, the papaya is about where avocados were ten or fifteen years ago."

In years to come, many other fresh fruits and vegetables may be transported by air from the areas where they are grown to major markets. But there will have to be some changes.

The way it is now, cantaloupes, grown in Arizona and California, are packed in crates and shipped by rail to Eastern cities. But there is a great deal of waste to a cantaloupe, and every time a shipper pays the freight on a carload of cantaloupes, he also happens to be paying the freight on almost a carload of garbage.

Before leaving the growing centers of the West, cantaloupes will be peeled and their seeds removed. They will then be cut into portion-size wedges, packed in lightweight plastic containers, and shipped overnight by airfreight to Eastern customers. Some experts believe that this system would so increase the attractiveness of the product, in terms of both eye appeal and convenience, that the consumption of cantaloupes would probably double.

Asparagus is another product that could be shipped by air—if the asparagus waste was left in California. The inedible woody portions of the stalks represent about one third of the fresh asparagus that is now being shipped across the country. This also applies to broccoli; about one half of every bunch of broccoli winds up in the garbage pail.

The same kind of planning can be applied to other commodities. Take

A modern jet freighter

beef, for instance. It requires three or four days for a freight car of beef to reach New York City from Kansas City, then another two or three days for the beef to be distributed to the retail outlets and restaurants. During this time the product may lose as much as 5 percent of its weight in shrinkage, which represents a significant financial loss to the shipper.

As a result, there is a growing trend toward shipping beef by air. But instead of quarters of beef being shipped, which is now the custom, the product will be cut and packaged into consumer-size units at the distribution center. No longer will the job be done in the back room of the supermarket.

By leaving the bones and excess trimming at the processing plant, the shipper will be able to afford the higher rates of air transportation. And he won't have to bear the losses that result from shrinkage.

Many foreign countries represent a potential for the air-cargo industry. In Chile, for example, where seasons are the reverse of what they are here, asparagus ripens in September and October. Sweet cherries can be harvested in November and December. The pick-ing of tree-ripened peaches begins in December.

Only a trickle of fruits and vegetables from South America reaches American markets now. The possibilities are exciting. It has been estimated that Chile alone has a production potential for fruits and vegetables that would make it the equal of California and Arizona combined.

Despite the fact that annual air-cargo movements are expressed in terms of billions of dollars, the industry still has only a minute share of the total market. The lion's share goes to trucks and trains. If the airfreight industry should continue to grow at current rates, the airlines will be carrying 0.4 percent of the total common carrier freight tonnage by 1975, and 1.9 percent by 1985.

Obviously, then, there is great potential for growth. In terms of perishables, this means that Oriental vegetables and fresh shrimp netted off the coast of Japan may begin appearing on our dinner tables. It means that we'll be enjoying Chilean peaches and occasionally a sweet, rich torte from Old Vienna. It means that the exotic may become commonplace.

8

UNIT TRAINS;
FULL SPEED AHEAD

SOME PEOPLE compare the unit train to the conveyor belt because it transports bulk shipments from one point to another in a continuous stream. Others say that it is the railroad's answer to the pipeline.

The unit freight train is not exactly a new idea in railroading—indeed, it was first used in the 1920's. But in recent years, thanks to the development of specialized railroad cars, more powerful locomotives, computerized car sorting, and a host of other advances, the concept of the unit train has reached its peak.

Unlike a conventional string of freight cars, which carry a wide variety of goods, the unit train is devoted to handling only one commodity. And it moves continuously from one city to another—bringing a load, depositing it, and then returning for another.

Normally, the use of locomotives to pull empty trains causes railroad men to shudder. Empty cars are not earning any money. But in the case of unit trains, it is different. Even though the cars are empty on the return trip, there is an overall improvement in efficiency in equipment use.

More than 2,500 unit trains are operating today. They cover round-trip routes ranging from 30 miles in dis-

This 66-car unit train carries molten sulfur from Rustler Springs, Texas, to Galveston

SANTA FE RAILWAY

tance to more than 5,500 miles.

In the past, unit trains have hauled only bulk materials—coal, iron ore, or grain. But in recent years they have begun to transport almost anything that must be conveyed in large volume between two points.

A steel company was able to build a new plant without any steelmaking furnaces, thanks to the unit train concept. Bethlehem Steel's Indiana plant, which turns out two million tons of finished steel a year, gets its steel slabs from Bethlehem's plant in Lackawanna, New York, 500 miles away. The slabs are hauled in unit trains that are often 100 cars long. Each is especially equipped to keep the steel hot, ready for fabrication.

Another unusual unit train is at work in the field of environmental improvement. It handles the delivery of Chicago's organic wastes to farmlands to the north, to the south, and to the west of the city, where they are used to enrich and restore the soil.

Huge quantities of fully digested and aged organic fertilizer are processed and stored in lagoons by the Metropolitan Sanitary District of Greater Chicago. At one location, 3,000 tons of wastes, reduced to a thin liquid, are pumped through a pipeline at a rail loading site and into specially lined tank cars. Then the cars containing this slurry are moved by train to a farm region where it is restored to the soil.

Chicago is only the beginning. It is expected that the system will be applied to other metropolitan regions,

About 40 percent of all coal shipments are made by unit trains

or to any region where organic wastes pose a problem to the population or to an industry.

The automobile industry has been extremely successful in using unit trains. General Motors Corporation, for example, the nation's largest auto manufacturer, operates six unit trains to speed delivery of its cars from assembly plants to dealers.

One of these unit trains covers a run that stretches from Chicago to Los Angeles. The train is empty as it begins in Chicago. It is broken up and the cars distributed to more than twenty different points in Michigan for loading. Then the train is reassembled and hauled as a unit to California.

Just before its arrival in Los Angeles, it is split into two parts. One section carries finished automobiles to Los Nietos for distribution to dealers, while the other transports parts to an assembly plant in Van Nuys. The two

75

sections of the train are reunited for the return trip to Chicago, where the cycle begins again.

The complete operation involves 6 different railroads. From start to finish, the trip takes 16 days. Before the unit concept was introduced, delivery took 50 percent longer.

Time is a vital factor in the delivery of new cars. The longer it takes to ship an automobile, the more likely it is that the automobile will arrive in a damaged state. Before the unit train idea was introduced, dealers in Chicago found that from 25 percent to 50 percent of the cars arriving from assembly plants in Kansas City were in less than factory-fresh condition. Much of the damage was caused by vandalism incurred during the trains' slow passage through the railroad yards in both Kansas City and Chicago.

The solution was a unit train that bypassed the railroad yards, going directly from the assembly plants to the unloading ramps. The train reduced transit time from four or five days to less than two and one half days.

Railroads also use computers to help keep automobile shipments moving fast. Since 1970, computers have monitored flatcars hauling automobiles in racks, and boxcars carrying parts. When a car fails to follow the route and the time schedule established for it, the computer lets people know. The wayward car is flagged down and steered back to its proper route.

To reduce damage to automobiles even further, railroads are working closely with auto manufacturers to develop railroad cars that will help to protect automobiles from vandals and thieves. "The idea," says a railroad executive, "is to keep cars out of the sight of—and, thus, out of the minds of—those bent on inflicting damage." This thinking has been incorporated in two new types of railroad cars that enclose automobiles in cocoonlike fashion.

One of these railroad cars is called Vert-A-Pac, the other Stac-Pak. Unit trains using these cars are already in operation.

The Vert-A-Pac car hauls 30 automobiles in a nose-down position be-

Rack cars are the traditional method of hauling new automobiles

Cars are loaded nose down when shipped via the new Vert-A-Pac system

hind metal sides. The sides are mounted to the car frame by heavy hinges, which enable the sides to serve as doors during loading or unloading.

While the use of a Vert-A-Pac car is limited to one particular automobile —General Motors' Vega—the Stac-Pak can handle a variety of standard-size cars. The Stac-Pak system consists of a tall, tiered metal container that is open at both ends. Each container is capable of carrying three automobiles, one stacked just above the other. Four such containers—twelve automobiles —ride aboard a flatcar.

Automobile manufacturers have traditionally shipped their cars in unprotected metal racks aboard flatcars.

Over the years, the industry has built up a fleet of 24,000 racks. Each has an estimated life-span of eight to ten years. As the racks wear out, they are likely to be replaced by carrying systems such as Vert-A-Pac and Stac-Pak.

The automobile industry isn't the only one to benefit from specialized freight cars. Countless other types have been developed in the past decade or so.

Some are easy to recognize, like the "snowy" refrigerator cars which derive their snowed-on appearance from a 2-inch exterior coating of insulation. Cars of this type are capable of carrying four times as much cargo as conventional refrigerator cars. The insu-

77

lated hoppers in which the cargo is stored eliminate expensive crating and packaging and help to reduce loading and unloading time.

Dry bulk materials, ranging from white flour and grain to cement and carbon black, are carried in cars with special pneumatic loading and unloading systems. These enable the cargo to be "inhaled" at the loading point and "exhaled" at the car's destination.

Reel cars, to transport the giant spools of cable used by the communications and power industries, are another recent innovation. These cars, some with carrying capacities of up to 180,000 pounds, transport reels of all sizes and weights, and some are equipped to permit roll-on, roll-off loading.

Grain is pneumatically loaded into a covered hopper

LOUISVILLE & NASHVILLE RAILROAD

The freight car classification yard at Chattanooga, Tennessee
SOUTHERN RAILWAY SYSTEM

Even the conventional boxcars have changed. They are much larger. Freight cars being retired have an average capacity of 61 tons. Those replacing them are about 40 percent larger, averaging 81 tons.

Modern freight cars roll better because of improved roller bearings. Other improvements include cushion-type underframes to give a smoother ride and wider door openings to permit mechanized loading and unloading.

The nation's railroads have traditionally pooled their freight cars, which has made it possible for one line to use the cars of any other line. Recently rail lines have also begun to pool locomotives. Pooled locomotive power means that freight trains, unit trains, in particular, are able to bypass

Cars are electronically sorted in modern freight car classification yards

interchange yards when moving from one railroad to another.

This new idea in railroading has led to the "run-through" train—so named because it "runs straight through" from wherever it originates to its destination. A run-through train pauses only for safety inspection, crew changes, and an occasional quick pickup—or delivery—of a preblocked section of cars. Run-throughs have enabled trains to cut their schedules for the run from the Atlantic to the Pacific Coasts by as much as 48 hours.

Most of the run-through trains now in operation were introduced during the early 1970's. Some railroads participate in as many as a half dozen run-throughs. The longest routes cover more than 3,000 miles. Some of the transcontinental run-throughs have daily departure schedules in each direction.

While the run-through concept has come into general use only in recent years, the idea goes back to the 1920's. The first run-through trains were "silk trains," used to speed Japanese silk from ports in the Pacific Northwest to markets in the East. This was before the manufacture of artificial fibers—nylon, orlon, and all the others—and Japanese silk was often valued at as much as $1,000 a bale.

Most silk trains were short, consisting of about ten cars. The very high value of the silk made it worthwhile to handle the shipments in run-through fashion. During 1929, the peak year, over 500,000 bales were carried.

Run-through trains and unit trains owe at least a part of their success to the computer and to electronic controls. Classification yards, where cars are sorted, have been almost entirely automated in recent years.

When a train enters an electronically controlled classification yard, automatic car identification scanners "read" color-coded labels on each car. Because these scanners can "read" extremely fast, the train can travel at 15 miles an hour, which is three times faster than it could travel when a man was doing the reading and writing down of the car numbers.

The scanner transmits the car numbers to a computer, which stores the information in its memory bank. The computer also stores the exact location of every car in the field. This information can be made available immediately to the man doing the sorting.

Suppose a train made up of cars bound for a variety of destinations enters a classification yard. The first step is to break up the train. At the same time, the cars must be sorted—"classified"—according to the final destination of each. The new trains, some of which are unit trains, then leave the yard in different directions.

The usual way to disassemble a train is to "hump" it. The train is directed over a man-made hill—the "hump"—which serves to uncouple the cars from one another. After being humped, the cars roll by gravity, each to its proper track.

A railroad man used to ride each of the cars. His job was to regulate the car's speed by means of a hand brake. Electronic controls have streamlined this phase of the operation. At the crest of the hump, an electronic scanner "reads" each car's number and transmits it to a television monitor in the yardmaster's office. At the same time, the computer automatically retards the car's speed to prevent it from damaging the string of cars it is to join. In order to do this, the computer has to calculate the car's gross weight, the distance it must travel, and the amount of curvature in the track.

Once the sorting has been completed, the computer prints out lists of the cars that make up each train. Another scanner checks the cars as the trains leave the yards. The computer to which this scanner is linked compares the new information with the previously prepared lists. If there is any discrepancy, the next station on the line is notified.

As a result of many of these innovations, today's trains are almost always longer than those of the past. Forty years ago the average freight train was 48 cars in length. Today, the average length is about 70 cars, and trains of 200 cars are no longer considered unusual.

This, in turn, has led to a new generation of diesel locomotives that are capable of providing horsepower in ever-increasing units. Although the locomotive is called simply a "diesel," the more accurate name is "diesel-elec-

Longer freight trains have created a need for their more powerful locomotives

"Land bridge" trains like this one, photographed near Kansas City, enable intercontinental shippers to bypass the Panama Canal

tric." A diesel engine is used to generate electricity which drives the motors that turn the locomotive's wheels.

The first trains were powered by steam engines, and, at the end of World War II, twenty years after the introduction of the diesel, steam locomotives still dominated the scene. By 1950, however, diesels had passed steam engines in number, 20,500 to 16,000. A decade later the steam locomotive had vanished from main-line use. About a dozen steam locomotives are still active today, but they perform no heavy duties.

The diesel-electrics were able to surpass steam locomotives because they were more economical to operate and required less maintenance. Another competitor, the all-electric locomotive,

has also declined in favor. There are about 300 all-electric locomotives in use today, about one third the peak number during the years of World War II. The principal disadvantage of the all-electric is cost; it requires heavy initial investment for the construction

82

A unit train, hauling a shipment of containerized freight that originated in Japan, rolls east through the Cajon Pass near Summit, California

SANTA FE RAILWAY

of transmission equipment along the right-of-way.

A modern diesel-electric locomotive can generate 3,600 horsepower. Most diesels of the 1950's were rated at 1,500 horsepower. While horsepower ratings have more than doubled, locomotive costs have gone up as well. Present-day diesels carry a $290,000 price tag. In 1957 the average unit cost about $157,000.

The evolution of diesel power shows no sign of abating. Even more powerful locomotives—some of 6,000 horsepower—are already in service. There are predictions that railroads of the near future may boast locomotives that are rated between 10,000 and 15,000 horsepower, perhaps to be powered by nuclear energy.

It is possible to attain power of this type today by the use of "booster" units. These are diesels coupled at well-spaced points within a long train. Not only does this system "boost" power significantly, it also makes for smoother braking.

More powerful locomotives, computerized car sorting, and unit trains that "run through" from one point to another have increased railroad efficiency to such a degree that many intercontinental shippers are coming to look upon the United States as a vast "land bridge." Cargo from Japan being shipped to the East Coast now is often loaded aboard railway flatcars in Los Angeles or Richmond, California.

The same is true for the other direction. Cargo bound for the West Coast from Europe is frequently transshipped by rail. The railroads haven't yet made the Panama Canal obsolete—but they are trying.

9

FROZEN ENERGY

G AS IS a premium fuel. It is clean, convenient, and cheap. Everybody wants it—homeowners, store owners, and power plant superintendents.

Gas supplies about one half of all residential and commercial heating in the United States. It furnishes one half of all the energy for industrial power.

But the United States is facing a gas shortage. As early as 1971, domestic gas producers were unable to meet the country's requirements. Importing gas is the only answer.

The principal sources of supply outside the United States include the Soviet Union (which has been endowed with an estimated one third of the world's known reserves), Iran, and Algeria. A pipeline from any one of these countries to the United States is obviously out of the question. The solution to the problem of getting the gas here has triggered a surge of activity at shipyards throughout the United States. That solution is the gas tanker.

Shipping gas by ocean vessel happens to be practical because gas has

the remarkable property of being convertible into a liquid. This is done by subjecting the gas to extremely low temperatures.

Liquefying the gas reduces its volume 620 times. In other words, 620 cubic feet of natural gas can be reduced to 1 cubic foot of liquid gas. Or look at it like this: The liquid natural gas it takes to fill a cigar box can be revaporized into enough natural gas to fill a telephone booth.

The gas is taken from the ground in its natural state, then liquefied and piped aboard ship. At its destination, the gas is stored as a liquid. It is revaporized when needed, then fed into pipelines and mains for distribution to consumers.

There are at present only a small handful of ships able to carry liquid gas. In order to satisfy the country's increasing demands for gas, U.S. maritime officials have estimated that 100 new gas tankers will be needed by 1980, and an additional 50 by 1985. That is seven billion dollars' worth of ships.

The first ship to test the special techniques involved in the transport of liquefied natural gas was of American design. In 1958, a World War II cargo ship was fitted with five boxlike aluminum tanks that were insulated with balsa wood sandwiched between layers of plywood. Christened the *Methane Pioneer,* the ship made seven voyages from the gas fields of Louisiana to England. The project was abandoned in 1961 when gas wells in Algeria went into production.

In the years that followed, other gas tankers were built in Italy, France, Norway, Spain, and Sweden. As of 1972, sixteen such vessels were in operation.

The *Esso Brega,* which has been transporting liquid gas from Libya across the Mediterranean to markets in Italy and Spain since 1969, is one of the largest and most sophisticated ships of this type. Its 4 huge insulated tanks hold 250,000 barrels of liquid gas, which revaporizes into 750 million cubic feet of natural gas. Three similar vessels are being built in Italy.

The gas tanker is often likened to a seagoing thermos bottle, but tankers have to insulate even more efficiently than any thermos ever did. They have to be capable of keeping the liquid gas at a temperature of minus 260° F.

A number of basic designs have been developed. American shipbuilders prefer what is known as "tank system" vessels. In these, the liquid is carried in several thick-walled spherical or cylindrical storage tanks, each one 120

The Brega *is one of four gas tankers to operate between Libya and European ports on the Mediterranean*

feet in height. These containers are made of 2-inch aluminum plate or nickel steel. The exterior is coated with plastic foam for insulation.

Other tankers employ one of two "membrane systems." In one of these, the ship's box-shaped holds are insulated with sheets of crimped stainless steel that have been backed with balsa wood and mineral wool.

In the other membrane system, tanks are constructed out of thousands of plywood boxes, each box about the size of a small suitcase. The boxes are glued together and then filled with perlite, a special insulating glass. The tank interior is faced with a thin layer of iron alloy, high in nickel content.

85

*Vessels utilizing the tank system to carry
liquid natural gas will look like this*
GENERAL DYNAMICS

Ships that use spherical tanks are less
expensive to build, but they cause
space to be wasted. Tanks based on the
membrane system use every bit of
available area.

On the drawing board is a third
type of gas tanker, one that would be
based on the LASH (*L*ighter *A*board
*SH*ip) principle discussed in Chapter 1.
This vessel would carry three huge
barges, each fitted with a spherical
liquid-gas container. The ship would
unload the barges at dockside, or drop
them off, one by one, at different
points. "The system works the same
way that was used for delivering milk,"
says a spokesman for a company interested in building such vessels. "You
drop off full 'bottles,' and pick up
empties."

American shipyards are said to be
better suited to the construction of gas
tankers than shipyards in foreign countries. The materials required to contain and insulate the liquid gas—
chiefly aluminum—are readily available here. And the United States,
thanks to the knowledge derived from
the space program, is the world leader
in cryogenics, the science that deals
with the production of ultralow temperatures.

Construction of three tank-system
vessels began late in 1972 at a Quincy,
Massachusetts, shipyard. Scheduled for

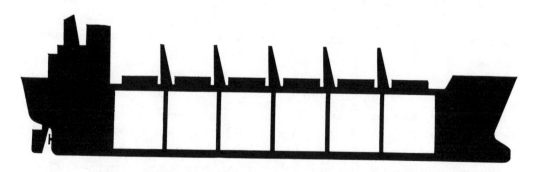

*Vessels using the membrane system have boxlike holds and
thus a greater carrying capacity than ships using the tank
system*

FEDERAL POWER COMMISSION

completion in 1975, these vessels will look like no others ever constructed in the United States. A row of storage tanks—five of them, each 120 feet in diameter—juts up from the main deck, making the ship look as if it is carrying a string of giant inverted mixing bowls. Each of these vessels will be 926 feet in length, as long as three football fields end to end.

Each tanker will be able to transport 125,000 cubic meters of liquid gas. When revaporized, this is enough gas to heat the homes and cook the meals of all the gas users in New York City for six days. Designs for tankers capable of carrying 200,000 cubic meters of gas have been completed. Vessels of this size may be in service before 1980.

El Paso Natural Gas, one of the world's largest gas transmission companies, plans to use a fleet of nine tankers in delivering gas from Algeria to the firm's terminals in Cove Point, Maryland, and Savannah, Georgia. Three of the tankers are being built in France; the six others, in America.

All nine of the vessels will employ the membrane system. In appearance, they will resemble oil tankers, a long, flat deck forward, the pilothouse aft. The first vessels of this class will be operating by 1975.

The problem of the nation's energy supply keeps getting worse. Nuclear power has not lived up to expectations, mostly because of environmental con-

Nine tankers of this type, using the membrane system, are being built for one gas transmission company

EL PASO NATURAL GAS CO.

siderations. Coal-burning fuel plants, with their sulfur oxide emissions, also cause environmentalists to fret. Oil reserves are drying up, and to such an extent that the Department of the Interior has already warned that gasoline shortages have begun to develop in certain areas. Because of the limited availability of dam sites, hydroelectric energy is not the answer.

Natural gas is one solution—thanks to tankers that can carry the liquefied natural gas.

10

THE BIGGEST BIRD

THROUGH ALL the modern history of the United States, trucks, tractors, helicopters, and field guns went overseas by slow surface transport. Not anymore. The world's largest airplane, the C-5 Galaxy, has revolutionized logistics, putting American equipment, supplies, and personnel within hours of any trouble spot, anywhere in the world. In operation since 1970, this plane now regularly spans the Atlantic and the Pacific carrying its enormous payloads. "Galaxy" is the name the U.S. Air Force has given the plane, but it has also been called "the aluminum cloud" or "the Holland Tunnel with wings."

In 1903, when Orville and Wilbur Wright made the first powered flights of a heavier-than-air craft, the distance covered was less than the length of the C-5's cargo compartment.

The C-5 Galaxy, the world's largest airplane

LOCKHEED-GEORGIA CO.

Aircraft	Length	Wingspan	Height	Weight
C-5	247.8 ft.	222.8 ft.	63.1 ft.	764,500 lbs.
B-747	231.4	195.7	63.5	680,000
Concorde	194	83.9	38	551,160

A comparison of the C-5 with other large transports

Or think of the C-5 in these terms: If you put the plane on a football field and lined up its tail with the goal line, its nose would be just inside the 20-yard line at the opposite end of the field. The tips of its wings would be well beyond both team's benches. The C-5's tail is six stories in height.

How fast does the Galaxy travel? What is its range? The answers to these questions depend upon how heavy a load the plane is carrying. For example, the C-5 can easily deliver a 100,-000-pound payload 6,325 miles at a speed of just over 500 miles an hour.

Loaded to more than double that weight—220,000 pounds—it can cover 3,105 miles at the same speed. But reduce the payload slightly—from 220,000 to 200,000 pounds—and the C-5's speed will increase to 530 miles per hour over the same distance.

Its remarkable range makes the Galaxy particularly valuable in resupply missions. For instance, the plane can fly 2,875 miles with a 100,000-pound payload, unload, and then, without stopping to refuel, continue for another 2,875 miles.

On June 30, 1968, the Galaxy flew for the first time. Test pilot Leo G.

Sullivan, commanding a crew of five, eased the huge plane with its great, gray wings down the runway and into the air at Dobbins Air Force Base at Marietta, Georgia, steered over the green-forested countryside, and then returned for a gentle landing 94 minutes later.

"It flew beautifully," said the pilot as he emerged from the forward

Six buses, with plenty of room in between, fit beneath a wing of the C-5. All six buses will easily fit also inside the plane

LOCKHEED-GEORGIA CO.

hatch. "It couldn't have been nicer."

During the early 1970's, the C-5 became a well-known international figure, regularly spanning the Atlantic and the Pacific. Some of its recent achievements include:

1. Taking off with a weight of 798,-200 pounds, a world record.

2. Attaining an airspeed of 611 miles per hour.

3. Flying 20 hours, 36 minutes, nonstop and without being refueled, from Edwards Air Force Base, California, to Seattle, Washington, to Bangor, Maine, and then back to California.

4. Navigating across the Arctic tundra to the North Pole and flying "around the world" in 4 minutes.

5. Unloading 36 pallets of cargo

The largest payload ever placed on an airplane, 257,000 pounds, was unloaded from this C-5 in about 15 minutes
LOCKHEED-GEORGIA CO.

weighing some 257,000 pounds in about 15 minutes.

6. Regularly landing, from point of touchdown to a full stop, in only 1,200 feet.

All this is fine, but what makes the

This string of 23 vehicles made up one load for the C-5
LOCKHEED-GEORGIA CO.

Galaxy the darling of U.S. military planners is its ability to transport any and all types of equipment used by an Army division. This includes such items as an armored personnel carrier (21,590 pounds), a 175mm. self-propelled gun (61,200 pounds), plus the Army's M-60 tank, its main battle tank (105,500 pounds).

In a single 72-hour round-trip flight, a C-5 delivered three big Army twin-engined Chinook helicopters, with only the rotors removed, to Vietnam, and brought back three battle-damaged Chinooks to the United States for repairs. Had smaller transport planes been used, it would have been necessary to disassemble the helicopters in the United States and put them together again in Vietnam. Not only would this have required the services of several mechanics over an 8-day period, but it would have taken three separate smaller transport planes.

When the National Aeronautics and Space Administration wanted to get the first-stage booster of an Atlas missile from California to Cape Kennedy, Florida, it requested a Galaxy. The giant plane swallowed the whole thing.

The Galaxy is also noteworthy because it can airdrop, that is, deliver men and supplies by parachute. Two jump platforms, one on each side of the fuselage, permit paratroops to make their exit.

Loading the Galaxy is a cinch. It is like an enormous aluminum tube with a cargo opening at each end. The nose opening lifts straight up like the visor

Outsize loads like this 62,000-pound Atlas missile are no problem for the C-5
LOCKHEED-GEORGIA CO.

on a knight's helmet. When fully raised, it clears the cockpit windshield so as to give the pilot visibility should he need to taxi the plane. Whatever goes in the front end can exit at the rear, where there is another cargo opening of equal size.

Each opening is serviced by an adjustable loading ramp which is stowed aboard the plane. Each ramp is wide enough to permit three jeeps abreast to chug aboard. And as for strength, each ramp can support weights in excess of 100,000 pounds.

When the C-5 is landing or taking off, the main deck is 8¾ feet off the ground. To facilitate loading, the deck can be lowered by almost three feet. Landing-gear motors drive ball screws that lift the entire airplane up or down

91

over a range of 32 inches. "This plane is like a camel," says an official of the Lockheed Aircraft Corporation. "It kneels."

This system also enables the loading deck to be tilted forward or backward. Or it can be adjusted in either direction laterally to compensate for a slope in a taxiway or parking area.

The Galaxy was designed to work, to stay in the air, not to sit in a maintenance hangar. It is one of the easiest planes to service in the history of aviation.

A unique system of fasteners enables mechanics to replace any one of the aircraft's four turbofan engines in less than an hour. (A turbofan is a type of jet engine in which a fan forces air diverted from the main engine into the hot turbine exhaust. Engines of this type are capable of generating greater power and thrust than less sophisticated jet engines.) Engine fuel pumps have been so designed that they can be removed and repaired without draining fuel tanks, thus greatly reducing maintenance time.

The plane's enormous size helps to speed maintenance chores. For example, inspection of the C-5's tail assembly can be performed from *inside*. Lighted passageways equipped with ladders in the vertical fin and crawl spaces inside the horizontal stabilizer allow service personnel to check or to repair the various tail components. And they can perform such chores while the plane is in the air.

Refueling is another high-speed op-

The C-5 is the only plane in the world large enough to airlift the Navy's biggest helicopter, the Sea Stallion
LOCKHEED-GEORGIA CO.

eration. Through its four refueling ports, the Galaxy can gulp down its 49,000 gallons of fuel in about forty minutes. That's enough fuel to fill six standard-size railroad tank cars easily.

But the greatest contribution toward ease of service and maintenance is a remarkable electronic watchdog that monitors the aircraft from nose to tail, from wingtip to wingtip. It's called "madar," an acronym for *mal*function *detection, *a*nalysis, and *r*ecording system.

Like a cardiograph that records the mechanical movements of the heart, madar keeps an electronic watch over more than 1,200 test points throughout the airplane. It reports the operating condition of each part to the flight engineer by means of an oscilloscope, an electronic instrument that functions in much the same way as the picture tube of a television set. The oscilloscope provides the "viewer" with an electronic squiggle called a wave form.

The flight engineer compares this wave form with sample squiggles from a memory bank which he projects onto the screen of a second oscilloscope. By comparing the two visual displays, he can tell whether or not a part is operating properly.

Madar not only discloses where the trouble spot is located and diagnoses the malady but it also reports the name and number of the malfunctioning part. The flight engineer can then check whether there is a spare part aboard. If there is none, he can radio ahead to the plane's destination and request that the part be ordered and waiting.

Madar is on the job continuously throughout the flight. Besides reporting its findings by means of the oscilloscope, it also produces a printed record. At the end of the flight, this is turned over to maintenance personnel for review.

There is one other amazing aspect of the Galaxy's talent for self-examination. The plane can weigh itself. Electronic devices installed in each landing gear send signals to a computer that produces information as to the gross weight of the aircraft and the location of the center of gravity.

Crew members simply take a weight reading for the whole plane before the cargo is placed aboard, then a second reading after it has been loaded. The system can also be used to figure the weight of individual pieces of cargo.

Another remarkable feature of the Galaxy is its 28-wheel landing gear. The main gear consists of four 6-wheel sets. Each set is called a "bogie." In addition, 4 wheels arranged abreast are mounted at the nose.

The use of so many wheels serves to distribute the enormous weight of the plane over a large area, and as a result the craft treats runways gently. It is no more of a burden than much smaller planes. In fact, the C-5 can even be landed on dirt runways.

While airborne, the flight engineer can prepare for a landing on a dirt strip by deflating the tires slightly. If you were to try to ride a bicycle with slim, solid rubber tires over loose earth, you would sink in. But with big balloon tires on the bike, you would go right through. The same principle applies to the Galaxy, with the flight engineer adjusting the air pressure to suit the landing surface.

Of course, the Galaxy, and big planes in general, can't land on sand or loose soil. The runway has to be at least as hard as a baseball infield.

The fact that each bogie has its own control system facilitates landing-gear maintenance. If a tire needs changing or brakes require servicing, the bogie involved is raised. The plane stands solid and stable on the three other bogies and the nose gear while the mechanics work.

Planes today are constructed of aluminum, and the Galaxy is no exception. Its structural parts and exterior skin are made up of about 225,000 pounds of aluminum. There are also 50,000 pounds of high-strength steels within the plane.

In addition, it contains large quantities of some of the more exotic metals and alloys. Titanium, for instance. A remarkably strong, lightweight, corrosive-resistant metal, titanium is used instead of steel in about 65 percent of the C-5's more than 2 million fasteners. In total, the Galaxy requires about 8,300 pounds of titanium.

Beryllium, another metal that is extremely light in weight, was used in combination with other metals to create an alloy from which the C-5's brakes were manufactured. Steel is usually used for aircraft brakes, but beryllium, engineers found, cut down on weight and at the same time gave greater braking efficiency. Magnesium castings were used at dozens of points throughout the plane, and 1,000 pounds of depleted uranium went into the plane's control systems as counterbalances.

Although the Galaxy has come to be regarded as one of the wonders of modern aviation, it has proved a very costly one, too costly say some members of Congress. Cost overruns—development and manufacturing costs above and beyond the original contract figures—inflated the price of the plane.

Originally, the Air Force planned to purchase 120 C-5's at an estimated cost of $3.4 billion. The order was later cut back to 81 planes, and for these the Air Force paid approximately $4.4 bil-

94

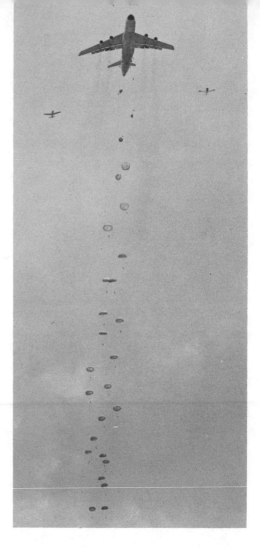

As the C-5 performs an airdrop, escort planes underscore the cargo giant's enormous size

lion. All 81 aircraft were in operation by mid-1973.

There were some design problems, too, particularly with the landing gear and the plane's ability to "kneel." One Lockheed official shrugged off the difficulties. "We may well expect to have other problems too," he said. "After all, the C-5 is a substantial jump in the state of the art. But as other difficulties occur, we'll fix them."

One of the "other difficulties" took place during a takeoff in Oklahoma in 1971, when an engine fell off. All C-5's in operation were temporarily grounded so that technicians could make structural modifications to strengthen the plane.

Such problems are part of the plane's development history now. Pilots who fly the Galaxy shout its praises, and Air Force officials hail the aircraft for doing everything it is asked to do.

In years to come, the C-5 may make obsolete all present ideas about civilian air travel. Converted to passenger use, a Galaxy could possibly carry as many as a thousand passengers at fares well below current levels.

But even if it never hauls a single paying passenger, the Galaxy remains one of a kind. For carrying massive loads of equipment and supplies across the world, no other transportation system can compare with it.

BIBLIOGRAPHY

Chapter 1   THE BIG STEEL BOX

Analysis of World Tank Ship Fleet. Philadelphia: Corporate Development
   Group, Sun Oil Company, August, 1971.
"Exploding Supertankers," *Time,* January 25, 1971.
"A Giant Alternative to the Suez Canal," *Fortune,* August, 1971.
"No Superports for Supertankers," *Business Week,* May 20, 1971.
"Racing to Build Supertankers," *Business Week,* August 7, 1971.
Safer Tankers and Cleaner Seas. Exxon Background Series, No. 3, Novem-
   ber, 1971.
"Superports-Superproblems," *The National Observer,* August 26, 1972.
"Surge of Orders Relaunches the Shipyards," *Business Week,* January 10,
   1970.
The Tankers Are Coming. Standard Oil Company (N.J.) (no date).
"U.S. Boom Coming in Ships to Haul Gas, Oil," *U.S. News & World Report,*
   September 4, 1972.
"World's Largest Ship Delivers 120-Million-Gallon Payload of Oil," *Popular
   Science,* July, 1972.

Chapter 2   FIRST STEPS TOWARD SPACE

"Apollo 17 Rolled to Launching Pad," *The New York Times,* August 28,
   1972.
The Kennedy Space Center Transporter. National Aeronautics and Space
   Administration (no date).
Marion 630. Marion, Ohio: Marion Power Shovel Company, Inc. (no date).

Chapter 3   THE SEA GIANTS

Arctic Ship Offloading, S-64 Ship to Shore Concept. Operations Report.
   Sikorsky Aircraft, April 30, 1970.
"Barge Carriers Bid for Lost Sea Trade," *Time,* March 15, 1971.
"Containerization's Success Creates Problems," *Industry Week,* September 18,
   1972.
"LASH Ship Carries a Load of Irony," *The New York Times,* October 12,
   1969.

"The Maritime Industry's Expensive New Box," *Fortune,* November, 1967.
Sea Notes. (Historical Issue.) Sea-Land Service, Inc., August, 1972.
"A Showcase for Integrated Transport," *Business Week,* November 27, 1971.
  Newark-Elizabeth Complex.

Chapter 5   ON A LAYER OF AIR

"Air Cushion Cargo Craft Tested in Canada," *Aviation Week & Space Technology,* December 20, 1971.
"Bigger Role for Hovercraft in World's Navies Is Forecast," *The New York Times,* September 27, 1971.
Cagle, Rear Admiral Malcolm W., *Flying Ships: Hovercraft and Hydrofoils.* Dodd, Mead & Company, Inc., 1970.
"Drive for a Modern Navy—Warships That Fly," *U.S. News & World Report,* December 6, 1971.
"Flying the English Channel: Altitude 7 Feet," *Popular Mechanics,* January, 1969.
"Hovercraft Military Market Emphasized," *Aviation Week & Space Technology,* June 7, 1971.
Strike in the Arctic! Standard Oil Company (N.J.) (no date).
"Surface Effect Ships; Will They Become Our Zippy New Navy?" *Popular Science,* July, 1971.
Voyageur. Great Bend, Ontario: Bell Aerospace Canada, 1971.

Chapter 6   MODERN NOAHS

Animals and Animal Products, Subchapter D, "Exportation and Importation of Animals and Animal Products." Agricultural Research Service, U.S. Department of Agriculture, February, 1971.
Gresh, Harry, *The Animals Next Door.* Fleet Academic Editions, 1971.
Johnson, James R., *Zoos of Today.* David McKay Company, Inc., 1971.
"New Jersey's Drive-in Zoo," *The New York Times Magazine,* June 28, 1972.
Perry, John, *The World's a Zoo.* Dodd, Mead & Company, Inc., 1969.
"Southern White Rhinocerous, Translocation to the San Diego Wild Animal Park," *ZooNooz,* May, 1971.
Trefflich, Henry, and Anthony, Edward, *Jungle for Sale.* Hawthorn Books, Inc., 1967.
Zeehandelaar, Frederik J., and Sarnoff, Paul, *Zeebongo.* Prentice-Hall, Inc., 1971.

Chapter 7   FOOD'S MAGIC CARPET

Air Cargo from A to Z. Information Services Department, Air Transport Association, May, 1971.
"Computer and Container Called Keys to Air Freight," *The New York Times,* May 11, 1972.
"Innovations in Marketing Perishable Foods by Air," Fourth International Shipping and Containerization Exposition and Congress, Oakland, Calif., September 13, 1971.
Irwin, A. A., *Flying Perishables.* Phoenix, Ariz.: Irwin Associates, May, 1969.
Rhoads, W. R., "Air Cargo—The Future." Lockheed-Georgia Company, Marietta, Ga., May 15, 1969. (Speech.)

747F Freighter. Everett, Wash.: The Boeing Company, Commercial Airplane Group, January, 1971.

747, General Description. Everett, Wash.: The Boeing Company, Commercial Airplane Group, November, 1971.

Chapter 8   UNIT TRAINS; FULL SPEED AHEAD

Railroads Now. Washington, D.C.: Association of American Railroads (no date).

"Safe, Fast Transport for New Autos," *Railway Age,* September, 1972.

Yearbook of Railroad Facts, 1972. Washington, D.C.: Association of American Railroads.

Chapter 9   FROZEN ENERGY

"Conference Report," Liquid Natural Gas Conference, 1972, Shipbuilders Council of America. U.S. Maritime Administration.

Frozen Energy from Libya to Europe. Esso Middle East, a Division of Standard Oil Company (N.J.) (no date).

"Gas Tankers Buoy Shipyard Hopes," *The New York Times,* September 17, 1972.

"LNG Tankers Inflate Shipbuilders' Hopes," *Business Week,* August 19, 1972.

Chapter 10   THE BIGGEST BIRD

"Biggest Airplane Ever Built," *Popular Science,* May, 1969.

"C-5 Galaxy Becomes an International Figure." Lockheed-Georgia Company, Marietta, Ga., 1972. (Speech.)

"In Service: The Biggest Plane Yet," *U.S. News & World Report,* December 29, 1969.

"Whatever Happened to the C-5 White Elephant?," *U.S. News & World Report,* June 19, 1972.

ACKNOWLEDGMENTS

Countless people provided source material and photographs for use in this book, and many of them checked entire chapters or portions of chapters for technical accuracy. We wish to take this opportunity to thank them.

Robert Antes
Sea-Land Service, Inc.

Bill Burk
Atchison, Topeka & Santa Fe Railway

D. L. Butts
Texaco

Thomas R. Cole
Commercial Airplane Group
Boeing

Barry B. Combs
Union Pacific Railroad Company

P. K. Connolly
General Dynamics

Donald G. Fertman
Sikorsky Aircraft

Edwin Flood
President
Shipbuilders Council of America

Joe W. Grotegut
Association of American Railroads

Adrian S. Hooper
President
Interstate Oil Transport

Sam Johnson
American Airlines

Charles F. Kreiner
Director, Public Relations
Bell Aerospace Company

A. H. Lavender
National Aeronautics and Space
Administration
John F. Kennedy Space Center

I. C. Lawhead
Supervisor, Technical Services
Marion Power Shovel Co., Inc.

James F. McCarthy
Air Transport Association

John H. McFall
El Paso Natural Gas Company

R. E. Martin
United States Lines

Richard V. Martin
Lockheed-California Corporation

Jack Murphy
Standard Oil Company

Jeanne O'Neill
U. S. Postal Service Headquarters

Ronald M. Powell
Office of the Postmaster General

Earl Ross
American Petroleum Institute

John P. Roth
President
Animal Transports, Inc.

Frank Taylor
Director, Public Information
Los Angeles Zoo

Carole Towne
San Diego Zoo

Paul F. Van Wicklen
Editor, *Via Port of New York*
The Port of New York Authority

S. J. Wornom, Jr.
General Dynamics

INDEX

103